Songs of Innocence and Experience

Songs of Innocence and Experience

Essays in Celebration of the Ordinary

Christopher de Vinck

VIKING

VIKING
Published by the Penguin Group
Penguin Books USA Inc., 375 Hudson Street,
New York, New York 10014, U.S.A.
Penguin Books Ltd, 27 Wrights Lane,
London W8 5TZ, England
Penguin Books Australia Ltd, Ringwood,
Victoria, Australia
Penguin Books Canada Ltd, 10 Alcorn Avenue,
Toronto, Ontario, Canada M4V 3B2
Penguin Books (N.Z.) Ltd, 182–190 Wairau Road,
Auckland 10, New Zealand

Penguin Books Ltd, Registered Offices:
Harmondsworth, Middlesex, England

First published in 1994 by Viking Penguin,
a division of Penguin Books USA Inc.

10 9 8 7 6 5 4 3 2 1

"A Father's Fear" and "Small Deaths Along the Way" first appeared in *The Wall Street Journal*. All other essays first appeared in *The Evangelist*.

LIBRARY OF CONGRESS CATALOGING IN PUBLICATION DATA
De Vinck, Christopher, 1951–
    Songs of innocence and experience : essays in celebration of the ordinary /
by Christopher de Vinck.
    p.   cm.
    ISBN 0–670–85294–5
    1. De Vinck, Christopher, 1951–   —Biography.   2. Poets,
American—20th century—Biography.   I. Title.
PS3554.E11588S64   1994
814'54—dc20   93-46251

Printed in the United States of America
Set in Bodoni Book
Designed by Cheryl L. Cipriani

To Roe,

with love

Acknowledgments

I would like to acknowledge, with deep gratitude, the following people who have given me their gifts of guidance and encouragement: May Sarton, Wendell Berry, Jim Trelease, Peggy Noonan, Mina Mulvey, Barbara Phillips, Paul Barry, Tim Ferguson, Tom Lashnits, Jim Breig, Bob Pfohman, Bob Miller, Elizabeth Gordon, Dorothy Rabinowitz, Bill Reel, Diane Ravitch, John Sloan, George Zitney, Robert Coles, Mary Piereth, Robert Heller, Eunice Kennedy Shriver, Sargent Shriver, Ginny and Dick Thornburgh, Henri Nouwen, Madeleine L'Engle, Sandra Costich, Mindy Werner, J.D. McClatchy, Virginia Duncan, Russell Baker, Rafe Sagalyn, Jack Sweet, and Fred Rogers.

Contents

Songs of Old Age

Songs of Death

Songs of Christmas

Songs of the Circle

COME! WELCOME! SING!

This is my introduction, written in grass
Taken from the sun and color green:
I am of the earth, a distant voice
Out of the mountains, I thought at first,
But after wind and rain I've reconsidered:
A moisture surely, so of the sea
And female, the texture of shells,
Their underside, their inside.

Call me single stone, call me poet,
My name is lost among human voices.
Call me Ra. Call me king,
Though I am no king but a collector of leaves
In autumn, keeper of my clean windows,
Though what I have been given
Is not what I have chosen:
Songs, weeping, hands clasped
With a stranger, you,
If you come for new songs
And old embraces, as
Old as the sea.

So let me be king of the windows closing
And opening to you as I lean out
And shout: "Come! Welcome! Sing!"

Songs of Innocence and Experience

Introduction

One afternoon when I was nine and old enough to know better, I was in the basement, playing with my father's tools. I found a piece of wood, picked up a coping saw, and pressed the wood flat under the palm of my left hand. The handle of the saw fit in the grip of my right hand. I began to cut into the wood.

As the blade of the saw quickly cut, I became more and more confident of my carpentry skills, until the teeth of the saw ripped a deep gash into my waiting left hand.

I remember nothing else about the incident, but I do remember that many years later, as I wrote on the Selective Service form at the draft board that I had a scar on my left hand, my father denied it was there at all. It is difficult for fathers to acknowledge any blemishes on their sons.

That small scar has been with me for over thirty years, evidence that there was an innocence long ago. We need to have physical proof that a distant time existed.

I read about Russian immigrants who came to this country carrying dried mushrooms with them.

I remember the house of my childhood, where I scratched the names of my brothers and sisters with a piece of corundum on the kitchen window. I nearly lost my thumb in the basement of that house when my brother and I were playing with an ax. It was the house of Christmas, the house of the swallow's nest on the front porch in spring. The yard is where I learned to distinguish a cat-bird's cry from the bluejay's, where I kissed a girl for the first time, where my father built a sailboat, where my grandfather planted roses.

A seventy-six-year-old Lebanese friend of mine sleeps in his parents' bed. "I have carried this bed with me throughout my life. It is the bed where I was conceived. I stand up each morning and kiss the bed's corner in thanksgiving to my parents for the life they have given me."

We are all faint images of our former selves, contemplating our changing faces in the mirror, all a little frightened, perhaps, but most of us capable of carrying on to a certain end with courage and faith.

When I am sitting through a long meeting or waiting to give a speech, I rub my finger over the little scar on my left hand.

We need to remember the innocence that was born deep inside ourselves, because it is there that we can maintain our center. We need to remember that this innocence is not drowned. We step into the world of experience with passionate intensity, and I believe it is this intensity that has the power to destroy the song of innocence in us, but this intensity is also where we manipulate experience and create poetry, families, bread, music, a neat hedge, a collection of photographs.

Art becomes dark and ugly if innocence is destroyed. Beauty, I believe, comes from our ability to maintain the song of innocence in harmony with the song of experience and create a balance between the two.

Time in our lives is spent between doing what is necessary and doing what is felt. If we boil water for tea and do not dream about the hot shapes forming in the steam rising toward the kitchen ceiling, we become quickly old and defeated. And if we spend a lifetime pursuing the stars, rejecting home, routine, duty, then we become drunkards or liars.

We should not spend half our lives pursuing a caress and the other half dulling the senses.

How we wear the stars of both our desires and our limitations upon our heads will define our nobility.

How we live between the extremes of innocence and experience will determine the quality and tone of the songs we sing during the ordinary times of our quiet lives.

Songs
of the
Fathers

CANTO I

I cannot paint red dye on my face any longer,
Crushed from roots of asters,
Gathered in faith according to my father's wishes.

Lines beneath my eyes do not
Retain their authority over my spirit.
I cannot, my people, be considered one of you.
I lift the stone in my hand and toss it at your feet.
It is my acceptance of my own beginning,
Loosened from the single mass, cut away perhaps
By the force of an earth tremor, or by a fall I took
Beyond the garden among the asters today:
I could no longer remain in present time,
But took what was left behind, a single voice
Calling out to my mother after I was stung by a bee
And wept between the pine trees and the daylilies.

I have felt the hint of moisture against my skin,
Grass, or wet leaves, a softness against my belly.
It was no longer asters with stems stretched out
But my brothers and sisters naked, playing Oberon,
Mermaids, little gods eating raspberries
As my father burned leaves and grass.
The smoke circled his legs
Like a magic lasso in a cartoon
As he stepped in and disappeared
Inside it like a fading night,
Or a worn photograph appearing and
Disappearing as he leaned against his rake, this
God or general watching over the ruins
Of a fire or of the fire to come
Upon the dry grass.

That is what I saw when I rose up from the flowers.
I wish to return where berries are sweet
And my brother lifts his stick above his head
And claims the garden and no longer feels the heat
As my father steps out and stirs the ashes.

A
Father's
Fear

One September, my young daughter, Karen, woke up in the middle of a Saturday night with severe pain in her right foot.

"Mommy, it hurts so much." I vaguely heard the commotion as I slid back into sleep.

The next morning, Roe spoke about Karen's difficult night, the pain in her foot. "Perhaps someone ought to look at it."

Our regular doctor didn't have Sunday-morning hours, so we thought it best to take Karen to the emergency facility on the highway. Twenty minutes later, I carried my daughter into the lobby of the small brick building.

After my wife and I filled out some forms, we were quickly introduced to a young doctor. X rays of the foot were taken.

"A simple bone chip," the doctor pointed out. "I am not qualified to wrap the foot. You'll need to see an orthopedic surgeon. He'll know if she needs a soft or hard cast."

Two days afterward, Roe stepped into the orthopedic surgeon's office with Karen and the X rays.

After the new doctor examined Karen's foot and looked at the films, he said to Roe, "There is something more here. It isn't a bone chip. The first doctor's diagnosis is an honest mistake. You see here?" The surgeon pointed it out to my wife. "This does look like a chip on the bone, but it is really quite normal."

Roe looked at the black-and-gray film illuminated against the light.

"But look here," the doctor continued. "Do you see this bone? It is much larger than the others in her foot. That concerns me."

And so began the very first time any of our children was threatened by a force beyond a mother's and father's protection.

"What does it mean?" Roe asked.

"I'd like to order some tests on Karen: a bone scan, a blood test, and an MRI."

"But what does it *mean*?"

"Well, that bone. It is abnormally large. There's a reason: an infection, a fracture, perhaps a tumor. These tests will begin to tell us more."

The tests told us more. The MRI indicated that her bone was not broken. The blood test didn't detect an infection. The bone scan pointed to the flare-up in Karen's foot. After three weeks of tests, the orthopedic surgeon looked at the results and urged us to take Karen to the Sloan-Kettering Cancer Center in New York City.

I will never forget the image of nine-year-old Karen walking through the hospital doors clutching the large X ray envelope against her chest.

"We really can't tell what is going on in Karen's foot at the moment," the new doctor told us after examining the X rays. "She will have to have a biopsy."

I thought a biopsy would be a simple needle inserted into the bone.

"I'd like to admit Karen on Monday," the doctor said. "I'll perform the surgery on Tuesday morning, and if all goes well, Karen can go home on Wednesday."

"Excuse me," I said. "What did you say? Karen will have to stay overnight?"

Not until I was home and Karen was in bed did I fully understand what was happening. The doctors suspected that Karen had cancer.

We live our lives in the rhythms of drama, between ordinary routines and sudden jolts. I had thought until this point in my life that I could protect my children.

The poet Derek Walcott said that he liked growing up in the Caribbean. Living so close to the sea as a child, he said, gave him a sense of things larger than he was out there, things vast and powerful.

There is no power on this earth greater than death. I am still foolish enough, or young enough, to believe I can fight death as it tries to press against my daughter. I was a madman, believing in my superior strength in opposition to so vast and powerful a thing, this cancer.

On the morning of the biopsy, an anesthesiologist stepped up to Karen's bed and placed a green surgical cap on my daughter's head.

As Karen tucked her long brown hair under the cap, the doctor told her she looked like a fashion model.

The only thing Karen had wanted to bring to the hospital was Penny, her new Disney Dalmatian plush dog with its pink name tag. Penny traveled with Karen through the admissions office. Penny sat on Karen's lap when the intravenous tube was thrust into her vein.

Just as the nurse began to push Karen toward the operating room, my wife reached over to take Penny, for we were told our daughter couldn't have anything with her during surgery.

"Oh, Karen can take Penny," said the nurse, with her beautiful Dutch accent.

As Karen was wheeled away from us, she waved, Penny tucked under her arm.

We all endure hints of anguish differently. I wanted to stop the play, send the director to lunch, take Roe and Karen home and forget the whole thing. I was able to teach Karen how to ride a bicycle. I was able to comfort her when she had a fever. I couldn't take her away from the surgeons.

Roe and I spent the longest two hours of our lives sitting together in the hospital lobby as we waited to hear the biopsy results. The morning sun pressed against us.

Finally, down the hall, I could see, among the hospital crowds, our doctor in his green surgical gown.

"It looks good. I saw no evidence of cancer, no evidence of a tumor or an infection. I think it is a stress fracture. The bone in her foot sustained a trauma of some sort. The bone is bent and her body thinks it is broken, so her immune system is simply trying to repair the supposed damage. We couldn't tell this without the biopsy. She's going to be fine."

Roe and I were allowed to be with Karen right after the surgery. Our daughter was curled up under a blanket. A mist of steam was pumped around her face.

"Is she all right?" I asked the nurse.

"She's fine. She's just waking up. The steam helps her. The doctor said your daughter is fine. We don't get much good news in this recovery room."

I pulled Karen's blanket over her bare shoulders, and there, on the other side of her little bed, I found Penny, wearing a green surgical mask and cap.

Roe and I celebrate and sing that Karen doesn't have cancer. We human beings ought to celebrate and sing in praise of men and women who devote their lives to a career so filled with stress, sadness and, sometimes, joy at Sloan-Kettering.

We can be grateful for the development of scientific research and discoveries, but let us not forget that someone took the time to tie a little hat and mask around a toy dog just so a child could wake up and smile no matter what the outcome of her test.

Vast and powerful indeed.

Hope

in the

Darkness

David was late for Cub Scouts. "Karen!" I called out. "Michael! Please get your shoes on. We have to drive David to his meeting!"

Roe was at work. Dinner was finished—tacos, probably. I can cook tacos and I can cook toast. I remember a conversation I had with a number of people at work. We were discussing income, husbands and wives both working, when I casually mentioned that on Tuesdays and Thursdays I give the children dinner.

"You cook the children a dinner?" someone asked, impressed that I attempted such a thing.

"Well, I don't really cook. I just take something out of the freezer and pop it in the microwave."

"That's cooking!" one of my colleagues said, laughing.

"Karen! Michael! David is waiting in the car. Come on, you guys!"

The two of them ran into the hall, grabbed their coats, and zoomed down the side steps and into the car. After I locked the door, I proceeded to the car. Opening the driver's door, I was greeted with wild hoots and shouts. "Stop the noise! You're driving me crazy!"

As I drove, the children sat in the back, poking each other silently, trying not to add to the tension. David groaned.

I pulled up to his troop leader's home, wished him a good time. "I'll pick you up at eight o'clock."

" 'Bye, Daddy. I love you."

"I love you too."

The car started rocking. Michael was jumping back and forth on the seat. Even Karen was beginning to be annoyed with him.

"Michael," I said. "I'm tired. It's been a long day. I expect you to calm down and help." He giggled. At certain times during the day, asking a five-year-old to calm down is like asking a crocodile to become a vegetarian.

The closer we drove to the house, the more Michael misbehaved.

By the time we rolled into the driveway, I was fed up. So was Karen. She hopped out of the car. I joined her.

"Well, I'm not getting out," Michael said triumphantly.

"Fine," I said, slamming the door.

It was six-thirty. The sun had set nearly an hour earlier. As I walked up the front lawn, then up the steps, I could hear Michael crying. I was so annoyed with him that I didn't turn around but simply stepped into the house.

"What about Michael?" Karen asked with true concern.

"He can come in on his own if he likes." I carried my annoyance into the kitchen, lifted the dirty dinner dishes from the table, and dropped them into the sink.

"But it's dark, Daddy."

I ignored Karen, turned the faucet on, squeezed dish detergent into a wide bowl, and began scrubbing a flat plate. Karen sat at the table.

I rinsed the plates, the glasses, the forks and knives. Everything was in the drainboard. I turned and watched Karen kicking her legs back and forth as she sat on her chair in silence.

As I began to dry the dishes, I looked out the window into the darkness. My anger suddenly turned into the tall oak tree in the distant backyard, as the shadows of the bushes crawled upon the grass toward the house as a car wound its way through the neighborhood.

"It's dark, Daddy," Karen said behind me.

I draped the towel over the back of the chair and stepped out the front door. There was Michael, sitting in the car. I could see his small head framed in the side window as the living room light illuminated his face.

I walked into the night, stepped up to the car, pulled open the latch of the door.

Michael looked up at me and whispered, "I knew you'd come for me, Daddy," and then he rolled into my arms.

Hope is knowing that salvation will come even as you sit in the darkness. Michael pressed his head against my shoulder as we walked into the house and the screen door swung shut behind us.

Fathers
and
Sons

"Each of you will be given a kit. Inside the box you will find a block of wood, four wheels, and two axles. You may not add anything except paint and decals."

So began the official Pinewood Derby competition in David's Cub Scout troop. That spring, he and I learned a lesson.

In the car on the way home from the meeting, David said, "I don't want to do this. I don't want to be in the race." His face was illuminated by the glow of the dashboard lights.

"Why not?"

"I just don't like doing these things."

David did not like to join things when he was nine. Perhaps he still doesn't. Perhaps he takes after his father more than I realized.

I never joined scouts, but I could swim across the Atlantic, climb the Alps backward, survive on the surface of Venus with a penknife when I was nine, or so I thought, and that has made all the difference.

"Well, David, you did want to sign up for the scouts, or at least you were willing to give it a try."

"Yeah, but I didn't know I had to enter a stupid race."

I spent my childhood avoiding races, teams, competitions, because I was afraid of failing, afraid of being noticed, afraid of being laughed at. I was the child picked last for every team in my gym classes. I was the teenager pinned to the mat within thirty seconds during the wrestling portion of physical education.

While I was driving home from work recently, I came upon a car that was moving at least ten miles slower than I was. I drove up to the car and stepped on the brake.

Have you ever seen an image that you cannot identify immediately, and then the more you look, the more that image takes on its real form?

At first I noticed an odd shape strapped to the roof of the slow-moving car ahead of me. A rug? A piece of furniture? A deer . . . a large deer tied to the roof. Its antlered head hung upside down. Its eyes were open. Blood trickled from its mouth and ran along the left taillight.

"Daddy, I don't want to build a racing car. I don't want to be in the race."

How do you explain to a nine-year-old boy that he will have to stand up against other men and women in the future? How do you say that human beings have an inner need to exert power over the powerless? How do you explain guns, war, hunting, to a child?

"I'll help you build the car," I said to David as we pulled into the driveway.

"OK."

A few weeks later, two nights before the Pinewood Derby, David stepped down to my basement writing room, with the kit in his left hand. I glanced up from the poem I was working on.

"Daddy?"

I looked at the blue box, then at the poem. I wanted to finish the evening's writing. I wanted to be alone; instead I turned toward David. "Let's see what's in the box."

We sat on the floor, David and I, and picked out a seven-by-one-and-one-half-inch piece of wood, the four black plastic wheels, and the silver axles.

"I don't want to build a racing car. Everyone is making a racing car."

I was pleased to hear that David was learning to be different in the face of conformity.

"Well, what do you suggest?" I asked.

"I don't know."

We took the wood and cut it into two uneven lengths: a three-inch piece and a four-inch piece.

"Maybe if we glued this small part on top of the other piece," David said as he manipulated the wood in his hand like a puzzle. "It looks like a truck."

"What type of truck?"

"A milk truck?" he asked.

That is what I thought too. David found white paint, gave the truck two coats, pressed the axles into place, and snapped the wheels on both sides.

"Something is missing," I said as David and I leaned close, nearly cheek-to-cheek as we examined his creation.

"A sign. I think it needs a sign on the side, something to tell people what it is." David ran upstairs, clumped back down with a blue marker in his hand. He lifted the white truck as if he were a giant, and carefully he drew in windows, doors, and a sign on either side of the truck: MILK.

The drive to the town hall two nights later was painful for David and me. He didn't want to go. He felt, after all, that a milk truck was a dumb idea. So did I. We both wanted to return home, but his scout leader was expecting him. The race's time slots were already assigned. We both felt trapped.

At the beginning of the evening, all the cars, perhaps fifty of them, were lined up on the table to be admired: red racing car, blue racing car; car with fire painted on each side; car with fancy numbers, yellow racing car, blue racing car. Milk truck.

In the middle of the evening, the competition played itself out.

Red racing car zooming down the wooden slot. Yellow racing car breaking all records. Racing car with fire; racing car with lightning bolts, its speed and grace marking it as a clear winner. Green racing car zipping down the chute. One milk truck shaking, bouncing, rolling, down, down, down . . . stalling halfway and disqualified in the first round.

The evening ended with the judge's decisions and the distribution of trophies: "Fastest car," the judge announced, "Charlie Weber and his yellow car thirty-three."

Much applause.

"Second place, Barry Henderson with his red car fifteen!"

Much applause.

There were trophies for the best-built car, the funniest car, the cleverest.

"And the final award goes to the Judge's Choice—the car that exemplifies the true Cub Scout spirit, a true boy's effort: David de Vinck and his milk truck!"

The biggest applause of the night. Well, what do you know about that, as Jimmy Stewart would say.

David and I sat in silence as we drove home that night with the trophy and the milk truck on the seat between us.

We both felt powerful.

The Face
of My Father

When I stepped inside the house one evening after work, the three children ran to the door with a greeting, and Roe quickly said, "Your father had a mild stroke."

After I gave each child a kiss, Roe embraced me. "I didn't know how else to tell you. He's fine. Mom just called. She's at the hospital. I thought you'd like to go."

Five minutes later, I was back in the car in the darkness. It was raining.

It is a long trip we take from our routines to the bedside of an ill parent. My drive was only thirty minutes. The windshield wipers clicked back and forth. Time. Time. Time.

I am not close to my father. His is a life immersed in books and dreams about sailboats on the Mediterranean. Some men wear their children around their necks. My father wears his children in his heart. I know that because that is what my mother said, but the heart is impenetrable if it is not open to laughter and the common day. My father laughs in his heart, but he does not connect with the common day. Flowers could descend from the sky like a blizzard, and my father would not notice. Ask him to name all the rivers in Europe, or to translate a Latin phrase—then he will speak.

I had seven dollars in my wallet, and just enough gasoline for the trip to the hospital and back.

Three years ago, my father had a severe stroke, but after surgery, medication, and good luck, he recovered completely. When he returned home and sat again in his chair, an open book on his lap, I could, again, pretend that I was still seventeen.

When I am home with my mother and father, I am swallowed up by the walls, the sound of the stairs creaking, the feel of the linen on the dining room table . . . all as it has always been . . . all as it ought to be.

For Christmas one year, I received a wood soldier that was a bank. His hat was black. His uniform was red. A metal key opened the hatch under the soldier's feet where you could retrieve the money.

I remember struggling with the wrapping around the present. My father leaned over me as I sat on the floor. His long fingers surrounded the gift as he gently pulled apart the string and the tape. His hand and mine together pulled out the wood soldier.

I quickly found a space in the hospital parking lot. Jumping out of the car, I popped open my umbrella and ran through the rain toward the main entrance.

"Could you tell me where my father is?" I asked the woman at the information desk.

"Who is your father?"

I nearly said, "You know—my father," but then I said, as water dripped off my umbrella, "De Vinck. Jose de Vinck. He came in through emergency."

"He's still in emergency. Just walk down the hall. Take the door after the third painting."

The walls were covered with distinguished men in suits.

As I walked through the emergency ward door, a nurse approached me and asked, "Can I help you?"

"I'm looking for my father."

One summer afternoon, my brothers and sisters dared me to

climb up onto the chicken coop roof. I climbed on the green fence, reached for the roof, stretched, and pulled myself up.

"There! I did it! Hey, you guys! Where are you going?"

They ran away, laughing. That is when I realized that I couldn't get down. I cried and cried.

The back door opened. My father hurried to the chicken coop, stood on the bottom portion of the fence. "Jump into my arms, Chris," and I jumped for my life, into my life. He carried me across the lawn, up the back steps, and into the house.

"Who is your father?"

"De Vinck. Jose de Vinck?"

"Yes. He's here. Take a seat. I'll be right back."

I sat in a blue chair, shook my umbrella a bit, adjusted my tie, and then my mother stepped from around the corner. She kissed me, concerned that I had come all the way through the heavy rainstorm.

"Papa is fine. This afternoon he had a phone call. When he went to answer, he couldn't speak. He just slurred the words. That is when I realized something was wrong. He said he saw white and couldn't read. I called the doctor, and he called the ambulance. But Papa is completely himself now. The doctor is in with him."

I stepped up to his room in the emergency ward. The door was open a crack. I could hear the doctor clearly. "You've had a minor stroke. You are fine now. We'll keep you here tonight and tomorrow for tests. This could be hints of things to come. We'll know more tomorrow."

While I was listening, I shifted back and forth in the hallway until I could see my father's face through the crack of the door. He couldn't see me. Only half of his face could be viewed at a time. I looked back and forth from one eye to the other, his cheeks, his chin, the sound of his voice.

My father. There he is.

In the Corral

One afternoon, I stepped into the garage looking for the rake. I like the smell of the garage, where we rarely keep the car. It is the place for bicycles, the wagon, an old table, and the smell of moisture and earth. The garden tools hang from the rafters and from the pegs nailed against the side walls.

I like to stand in the garage during a heavy rainstorm, enjoying that illusion of being afloat in something precarious as the waves of forsythia rock back and forth in the wind and the rain splashes against the driveway.

Usually the bamboo rake is hanging on a nail to the right of the garden clippers. I didn't find it there. Perhaps on the other side of the wall. Not there either.

In the far corner, behind the bag of potting soil, I found what was left of the rake: the pole disconnected from the wide fan of bamboo stalks; the bamboo stalks separated from one another, dangling from the curled wire that once held them together.

I believe that a rake when not used begins to disintegrate by itself—unless the children decided to use the rake as a witch's broom, or a horse, or to dislodge a balsa airplane from the top of the hemlock.

Often in our lives we approach a task that leads us to a new and unexpected enterprise. I picked up the tangled remains of the bamboo rake and carried them in to the kitchen table. A paleontologist probably feels the same thing I felt: Here's a scattered collection of bones waiting to be reassembled. Is it a tyrannosaurus? A brontosaurus? A pterodactyl? A witch's broom? A bamboo rake?

First, I reconnected the stick to the gathered tips of bamboo. The bracket and screw were still attached to the pole, but the nut was missing. It was useless to hunt in the basement for a nut. I am hopeless when it comes to keeping loose screws, nuts, washers, tools, pens, shoes, paper clips, magnets. They all disappear.

A nut. A nut. Where can I find a nut? I wondered. Of course. I stepped outside and returned to the garage, a pair of pliers in my hand. I climbed up into the loft and found the fertilizer spreader; then I located a nut attached to a screw on the right handle. I turned the pliers, loosened the nut, spinning it around and around the screw until it fell into my open palm. I have been taking screws and brackets and nuts from the spreader for two years now. I do not know why it hasn't yet simply collapsed, for there isn't much holding it together any longer. (I gave up spreading fertilizer three years ago.)

Back in the kitchen, I attached the bracket to the pole, the pole to the rake, the screw through the hole, and the nut around the screw after I reassembled the bamboo stalks through the steel wire.

"Hey, Daddy," Michael called out as he raced past me in the kitchen on his way to the bathroom. "You fixed my horse!"

A Father's
Privilege

Robbie Jones told me a wonderful story as we met outside
the library one evening.

Rob is the third Jones to run the hardware store in town. His
grandfather, his father, and now Rob have all kept the town together
with wire, screws, paint, and wrenches for nearly a century.

The hardware store is just north of the First Reformed Church,
across from the pet store, down the street from Salley Cropper's
bookstore and the florist.

Do you remember how Charles Schulz convinced us that
Snoopy has vast rooms and a swimming pool in his small doghouse?
I think Schulz created Jones' Hardware Store. If you need gaskets,
locks, glue, paint, wire cutters, flashlights, Rob has them all, in all
sizes, shapes, quantities. I bet that if you needed a boiler for the
furnace, Rob would find the exact thing somewhere in his basement.
I have watched Rob walk down those basement stairs for the past
fifteen years, and he *always* comes up with what the customer has
asked for.

I, and perhaps most of the town, have discussed the national
economy with Rob over the paint-mixing machine. He and I have
shared, over the years, the joys and struggles of being a father. We
shared the struggles of letting go of the past. (Rob and I are the
same age.) I have never asked him, but I bet he has a weekly

Friday-night poker game in the aisle of the store with some of his oldest friends. If he doesn't, he ought to.

I was stepping out of the library with David. He needed help with his fifth-grade report on the elements. As David and I walked down the concrete steps, Rob was walking up the same stairs with an armful of overdue books.

"It's no fun bringing books back on time," he said, laughing.

We all stopped for a few moments, Rob, David, and I. The conversation quickly turned to the fifth-grade project, to the middle school, to the adjustments David had had to make when he left the elementary school in September.

"I'll never forget," Rob said, "the first day my daughter Kerry went off to the middle school. I drove her down in the truck, which annoyed her. It's not the classiest thing to drive around town in.

"Well, as we were driving to school, Kerry turned to me and said, 'You know, Dad, now that I'm in the middle school, you don't have to give me a kiss anymore as you pull up to the building.' "

Rob stood there and smiled as he continued his story.

"So I just sat in the truck and kept driving. I didn't say anything. I pulled into the jammed parking lot. Kids were jumping out of the cars and walking toward the school across the way.

"Kerry turned to me, said goodbye, pushed open the door, and began walking across the lot between the crowds on her way to school.

"Then I stepped out of my truck, cupped my hands around my mouth, and in my loudest voice called out, 'Kerry Jones didn't kiss her father goodbye!'

"You know what?" Rob asked. "I can't understand it, but ever since that morning, Kerry gives me a goodbye kiss."

Fathers have certain rights. One of them is to hang on to their children for as long as possible. Kerry is a lucky young woman.

I am forty-three. My father is eighty-three. I haven't kissed him in over thirty years.

Songs
of the
Lost Girls

CANTO II

Second lesson: Understand the image of beauty.
Remember it is just an image, as thin as a candle,
As wide as sunlight, both divine . . . beauty wide,
Beauty thin; beauty ugly, beauty beautiful,
Never prepared for a dance under the moon.

False moon, a penny in my pocket easily spent,
Smooth and cold to flip between my fingers,
Easily forgotten.
Woman against my chest, beauty never, beauty's image,
Cold between my fingers, wide, open.

The sun will blind us. Enjoy the heat against your skin,
Admire the shadows:

Indirect sunlight does not burn, does not kiss,
Does not destroy when passion dreams of such destruction.

The Owl and the Pussycat

Michael wanted to build a canoe. After he saw a plastic cowboy-and-Indian set in the local toy store, he asked me if we could build a canoe, "A real one, Dad."

"When you are older you might build one."

That response didn't impress my son.

To dream about creation has been the pastime of kings, peasants, lonely men and women, and active children.

> The owl and the pussycat went to sea
> In a beautiful pea-green boat.

So wrote Edward Lear in his whimsical poem in 1871. I always liked the idea of an owl and a cat courting for a year and a day upon the sea in their boat in pursuit of an appropriate wedding ring.

When we see something we like, or someone we love, we usually reach out to embrace the found beauty.

I received a letter from Mary, a long-ago friend: beautiful, bright Mary. She was my colleague during my first year of teaching. I knew I loved her right away. She loved me too.

Mary was married to Bob, and I was engaged to Roe.

After that first year, I moved to another school district. Roe and I married. We began our photo albums, bought a two-bedroom house, celebrated the births of our three children. I painted the house twice, taught for fifteen years, wrote, slept beside Roe, listened to the children stir in the next room. I listened to the sound of the rain against the roof at night.

Over the years, I watched the skunk dig up the grubs and my grass in the backyard in the middle of the night when I couldn't sleep; I listened to the distant train passing, listened to the mail truck rattle up the street.

I'd like someday to calibrate the passing of time not with numbers and clocks but with the light that passes through the dining room window in the late afternoon, or with the customary sounds of the children running wild after supper.

I hadn't seen Mary for fifteen years. Her husband found my first book, brought it to her, and then she wanted to see me again. "I suddenly just wanted to reach out and hug you."

I think we all have friends who touched us in a certain way once, and those friendships stay intact no matter how infrequently each sees the other. That is how it is between Mary and me.

We met at a restaurant. We hugged. We shed tears and then we talked and talked. Mary told me about the sabbatical she was taking from teaching, how she had spent the first week of September at the Jersey shore. She spoke about her husband with such devotion and love I felt as if I were prying into her personal life. I told her about Roe, the children. We were not prying; we were giving over to each other what is best to exchange between old friends: all that has been lived and loved, with a hope that the other will approve.

After dinner, we walked along a small boardwalk that lined a half-mile lake. The sun set, the moon rose between the trees. We sat at a bench overlooking the lake, and the wind began to stir.

Mary and I confided our life victories: the love for our spouses, the daily struggles. She spoke about her teaching, her thirst to continue looking for answers and sustained peace. I spoke about my loneliness among those I love, the struggles of being a writer. The evening was a reckoning for both of us: These are the trails we have created. These are the lines we followed.

Mary looked at her sabbatical as a spiritual adventure. She was going off to a week with the Outward Bound experience. She had spent a week walking along the lip of the ocean, and she wanted to see me. It was easy to tell she had discovered who she was by virtue of her marriage, her career as a teacher, her recognition that the ocean possesses great power over her ebbing youth.

The owl and the pussycat went to sea.

When people's lives cross, when a spiritual bond is created between two people, that bond is rarely broken. That relationship —notions of love—ought to exist between a husband and wife, and it often exists between friends.

As we looked out across the lake that early evening, we both realized, or remembered, that had circumstances been different, we could have set forth together into that sea, sitting precariously upon that pea-green boat, but she and Bob have forged their love into an icon of marriage; Roe and I, too, have embraced each other in love, commitment, and joy.

I am glad that Mary included me in her quest for renewed energy and the sense of who she is. I am glad that she could trust me to be her mirror. In the reflection of those we love we see ourselves.

Maybe Michael and I will someday build that canoe after all. I have some large, empty cardboard boxes, and we can pretend that the basement is a wild river full of salmon twisting upward into the light, revealing their silver, smooth, wet, and beautiful bodies, forever elusive and impossible to catch.

The Dancer
and
the Deer

When I was twenty-three, I knew a ballerina, a true ballerina. We were friends. I met her at a seminar on American poetry at Columbia Univesity. I was a graduate student; she was visiting a friend, who brought her to a reading of William Carlos Williams's poems.

After the poems were read by various writing students, a discussion followed. Most people agreed that Williams's poems were clear, different, beautiful.

The ballerina said, "I like the way the poems make me think about how people move."

I asked her in the lobby of the auditorium what she meant by that. "The poem about a woman eating plums, and the one where a girl climbs over a rock wall and disappears, and the poem where the people slowly walk behind the wagon, carrying the coffin of a friend . . . Williams must have carefully watched the way people moved."

We continued our conversation out on the street, past the bookshop, past a florist. Our talk led to dinner and to an exchange of our lives: mine as a someday teacher and hers as a dancer.

Weeks led to months. The summer approached, and I was returning home. We planned to spend a summer night together at

Lincoln Center. I had never seen a ballet. She knew how many steps had to be climbed to reach our seats.

On the appointed day in July, I drove to Manhattan and met my ballerina, then we drove to Lincoln Center. After I parked the car, we walked through the hot evening air, passed between yellow taxicabs and regarded a fountain of white water rushing up into the darkness.

After the ballet, which left me mystified, we two were back on the street. The conversation was suddenly strained. I realized, or she did, that there could never be anything serious or lasting between us, after all. That is when it struck me that I had no idea where I had left the car. Somewhere over in that direction, on that street, perhaps over there?

How often have you driven to town, or to a mall, and simply left the car in the first available space? And how often do you forget the exact location of the car when you have finished your chores?

Well, my car was parked somewhere in New York City.

Do you remember when, in the film *The Wizard of Oz*, Dorothy, the Tin Man, and the Lion fell into a deep sleep after they ran through the field of poppies? And do you remmber how the Tin Man stood among his sleeping friends, lifted up his arms, and started pleading to any power that might be listening, "Help! Help!"

Well, try screaming for help in New York. But I did remember that Joan, a friend of my parents, lived down the street from Lincoln Center.

My silent ballerina and I walked to the apartment building. I buzzed Joan's apartment. She invited us upstairs.

"I lost my car."

Joan was happy to see me, was impressed with the beauty of my date, and laughed at my predicament. "We'll take my car, Chris, and retrace your steps."

May as well try to retrace Laurel and Hardy's footsteps in a desert sandstorm.

"How did you enter the city, Chris?"

"I took the George Washington Bridge." I knew where *that* was.

"Fine. Then where did you go?"

"Well, yes, I took the Henry Hudson Parkway."

Joan drove to the parkway exit nearby. "Yes," I said, "I came out here."

I sat in the back seat as Joan drove, and my dancer faded more and more into the closing curtains of a failed relationship.

It was simple. After taking this turn and that, remembering the street, a building, a theater, we eventually came upon my white 1968 Ford Falcon, sitting alone under a streetlamp like a naughty child.

I never saw the ballerina again.

While I was driving home from work some time ago, a deer leaped out from the left side of the highway, kicked her legs against the hard pavement, and flew into the air. I saw her smooth shoulder muscles, her eyes, the weight of her sleek body balanced upon the invisible force of gravity that seemed to hold her there, then, in my rearview mirror, the deer twisted upon the highway, mobilized her strength once again with confidence and elegance. She leaped back into the brush and tall grass and disappeared.

The second time I saw that performance, I thought, as I drove home.

The Mask of
Corporate
America

I once knew a girl with long brown hair. She had a soft cream tone to her skin, hazel eyes. She didn't like to wear makeup. She was nineteen.

We became friends. On many Sunday afternoons I rode my yellow bicycle to her house. We liked to ride north beyond her village, where a single store sold cheese, eggs, newspapers, and ice cream.

She always rode ahead of me. I liked to watch her hair collect behind her head as we zoomed down the long, steep hills.

"Do you know that I like to sing aloud on the first day of spring?" she once called out as she turned toward me and smiled. I remember the sound of her bicycle chain slapping against the metal frame.

I remember only a few things about this girl: She sat once on her living room floor and read aloud to me the poetry of Anne Sexton; baked me chocolate-chip cookies; spoke about a wooden chest in her bedroom where she kept all the things she had ever written, which I might be able to read someday. We walked together in our bare feet in a silver stream behind her house.

Sometimes we would stop at the distant store, sometimes we would not.

"Let's have cones. My treat," she said.

I liked the way our bicycles leaned together against the brick wall of the grocery store.

The hard ice cream was kept in large cardboard tubs lined up in two rows deep inside a white freezer: vanilla, chocolate, raspberry, sherbets, fudge swirls, heavenly hash, peach.

"I'll have chocolate." I always chose chocolate.

"Why aren't you daring? Try something new."

"Chocolate. I like that."

She ordered a scoop of raspberry and a scoop of peach.

If it was a very hot day, the ice cream quickly melted along the side of the cone. I was embarrassed as I tried to lick the sticky mess from my hands.

She enrolled in a New York City college; I began teaching. We lost contact. It is easy to let a friendship disintegrate.

Ten years later, I received an invitation to a wedding. My long-ago friend had a sister who was getting married.

I attended only the reception, which was held at the same house I had known.

The house was crowded. Cars lined each side of the street. When I stepped into the foyer, I was greeted by the girl's mother, who didn't remember me. I shook one stranger's hand after another as I wandered into the living room, the dining room.

"Chris." I heard her voice.

I turned and once again met my friend. I was deeply, deeply sad. She walked up to me in a crisp, fashionable blue dress. Her eyes were enhanced with makeup. Her hair was pushed up into a smart flip. She spoke to me about the accounting firm she worked for, about her fiancé, the fellow across the room who looked as if he had been born on computer printout.

I believe women should be paid the same salary as men. I believe women ought to pursue careers. I believe women ought to be ambitious. But I also believe women ought to retain their true beauty and not paint on the mask corporate America has so successfully placed upon the faces of men, business-suited warriors battling the competition, or the buyer, or the seller, or the supplier.

This girl had lost her beauty, just as those models we see in the flashy ads lose theirs: hair teased, skin smoothed with creams and color, eyes enlarged with black pencils and brushes, dresses that crisscross from shoulder to shoulder, mouths open, arms extended. I look at these models and I see a deep and troubling ugliness, something nearly beastlike.

I wanted to ask my old friend if she still sang aloud on the first day of spring, but someone offered me an hors d'oeuvre on a silver tray, so I didn't.

Sara

Perhaps I should have been a scientist. Instead, I became a writer. The vocations are similar in that they each demand keen observation. A scientist has to watch closely whatever it is that he or she is studying: the movements of the wind, perhaps, the change in the ocean floor, the division of molecules. After careful observation, a scientist makes a conclusion.

Writers do much the same thing. We walk around, poke our hands into the hands of those we love, we read the poets, taste the raspberries. Then we, well, step up to a sheet of paper and record our conclusions.

What is best to write about are those things that we have observed over a long period of time.

When I was thirteen years old, I met Sara. I had transferred from one school to another. On the first school day in September, I sat in the row near the windows. Sara sat in the row closest to the door. It was the first time I had seen her. She smiled at me. That was enough.

Sara and I have been friends ever since.

This is what I have observed about her:

a) On Memorial Day that first year, she stepped up to me as I stopped my bicycle near the parade route. She straddled the front wheel of the bike, held on to the chrome handlebars, swung back and forth, and laughed.

b) Someone painted "Sara and Chris" in a heart on the walls of the train station.

c) At the eighth-grade graduation dance, I finally asked Sara to dance with me at ten-thirty. The dance ended at eleven. I regretted not asking her at eight.

d) Her father drove a gray Ford. I looked for this car in the church parking lot each Sunday. Most of the time it was there.

e) In high school, Sara dated many boys. She and I had many, many phone conversations about her problems, my problems. We went to the movies together sometimes. I spent many, many evenings with Sara and her family. Her parents, signing my yearbook, called me their gypsy, for I came and went so often through their lives during my high school years.

f) Sara went to college. I did too. We exchanged a few letters.

g) She met a young man. Her father was dying of cancer. She wanted her father to attend her wedding. The wedding took place in her home in December; her father sat on the couch.

h) Three months after the wedding, Sara's father died.

i) Three years after the wedding, Sara divorced her young man.

j) Sara moved to New York City, was hired by a computer sales business. She became very successful.

k) Once or twice a year I'd call Sara; I'd send her a Christmas card; she'd write a one-line note saying that she wished me and my wife and children a happy New Year.

l) I hadn't seen her in nearly eight years.

m) During one of my visits to New York in connection with a book of mine, I thought that perhaps Sara and I could get together for lunch. We could.

n) She was, to me, the same girl who sat on my bicycle wheel twenty-seven years earlier.

o) We spoke about her work, about Roe and my three children. She spoke about her mother, her sister, her own life of lost loves, college courses she had just enrolled in, and then she simply started crying.

p) "I just wish I had a baby."

q) After we spoke in near whispers, she said, "I can't imagine why I said that. I can't understand why I said that."

r) She paid for the lunch.

s) This past Christmas, Roe and I received a card from Sara, wishing us a happy New Year.

I have tried to be the writer in my observations of this woman's life from the day she was thirteen until today. I remember her father before he became ill: tall, proud of his two daughters. When he smiled, the wrinkles in his face all turned upward, and you, too, would smile. I remember her mother laughing. I remember sitting at the edge of a small pond at the far end of Sara's property and how we two talked about her boyfriends, the war in Vietnam, teachers.

I still know her home telephone number by heart. I kissed her only once. I am past forty years old, and I have come to realize I do not have great powers of observation, after all.

A person can stand before you in all his or her strengths and weaknesses, and you will never know, really, what you are seeing. I have only small hints and conclusions about Sara's life: she has struggled, she is alone, she made choices.

Don't trust writers. They pretend to have a keener sense about what is going on in the world than most other people. A writer's conclusions are not scientific. A writer's conclusions are, at best, notes on the universe, sketches, scratches really upon the smooth surface of existence.

I think Sara ought to have a baby.

Songs
of the
Lost Boys

CANTO III

Third lesson: Do not accept salvation
In the form of colors or delights of summer
Created in memory against the promise of the sea.

Do not accept false images,
Thorns up the rose stem spread beyond the trellis,
Across the flagstones one by one.

I have seen them, country girls in bare feet
Discussing Cantafloss, the neighbor's son,
Enlarged with cancer, and how his skin felt
Against their pointed breasts one by one—
So he imagined them thinking
Each time a needle was pricked into his dead arm.

When Brothers
Become Men

When I was eleven, and my younger brother, Jose, was eight, we shared a room. My bed was against the east wall, at the foot of a window; his bed was at the west wall, at the foot of the other window.

One night as we lay in bed, we pretended that we didn't know how old we were. For some reason we thought this was funny. I remember asking Jose, "How old are you?" and he answered, "Eight, eight and a half—who knows?" And then we laughed and laughed.

One of Jose's most prized possessions when we were children was a red-and-white two-inch plastic owl that glowed in the dark. It was a key ring ornament, but to us it was better than the jewels of a kingdom.

I remember how we took the owl, ran to the living room lamp, placed the owl up to the face of the light bulb, and waited for the light to be absorbed in the owl's eyes and tail, the only portions of the trinket that glowed. Then Jose and I ran into the hall closet, squeezed ourselves between the coats and umbrellas, and closed the door. Jose slowly opened his closed hand. The owl's luminous eyes glowed an eerie green on his flat, open palm. "Lemme hold it?" I whispered, and he placed the owl in my hand.

After school one afternoon, Jose and I were sitting on the curb, waiting for a ride home. Local traffic rolled past us: cars, trucks, buses. Jose and I were tossing small bits of sand into the road.

At one point, a white truck drove by just as Jose was throwing a handful of loose dirt. The sand and small stones hit the side of the truck, and the driver quickly stopped, backed up, and hopped out. It was obvious he was angry. He leaned over Jose and me and demanded to know who had thrown the sand at his truck. "He did," I said, pointing as I edged away from my brother. The man screamed at Jose about the lack of respect, the cost of paint, then he walked back to his truck, slammed the door, and drove away.

I tied Jose to a pine tree once with a jump rope, ignored him in high school; after all, I was a senior and he was only a freshman.

I am forty-three. Jose is forty. He is a college English literature professor. Often he calls on the phone, or I call him, and we talk about books, wives, children, the cost of houses. Each holiday, we all return to our parents' house.

We are connected to our brothers and sisters differently than we are connected to our wives and husbands and children. We are always allowed to be the child in private moments with a sibling. I can still have a joust with my older brother in midsummer, our weapons dried daylily stalks.

Jose and I haven't squeezed ourselves into the closet together in over thirty years, but he still regrets losing the glowing owl. I regret not defending him against the truckdriver and ignoring him in the halls of the high school. I am not sure that I regret tying him to the tree, but at the Thanksgiving dinner table, or at the wedding table, or at the Fourth of July picnic, he'll look up from his plate of fried chicken and beans and smirk. "Eight, eight and a half— who knows," he'll say, and we'll laugh and laugh.

Bobby

Bobby was one of the tallest boys in my grammar school. In the summer his skin turned a deep brown. In the winter he played basketball.

I haven't seen him in more than thirty years, yet whenever I think about Huckleberry Finn, I think of Bobby—full of ground sense, a town boy who knew the best place to shoot off firecrackers without being caught (down by the abandoned pumphouse across the swamp).

Bobby taught me how to punch holes in tin cans, stuff them with dried leaves and straw, tie the cans to our bikes with a long rope, and set the contents on fire. The cans rattled and shook as Bobby and I zoomed through Main Street, leaving a trail of gray smoke behind us and an angry call from the mayor's wife or the dentist's wife—somebody's wife—wagging a finger. "Those boys!"

I remember walking home one summer afternoon with Bobby. We took the shortcut along the old trolley tracks, a narrow path, the town's spine, dividing east from west, and lined with backyard fences, wild roses, and blackberry bushes.

I remember how impressed I was with Bobby's feet. They were long and wide and bare. I would watch him take long strides in the path's beige dust. I never walked barefoot through town or along the deserted trolley tracks.

Once, Bobby and I each bought a bottle of Coca-Cola, the green bottles pinched at the waist. Bobby popped the metal cap off with his thick hands. I tried but cut my fingers along the serrated edge.

We exchanged sodas. After he easily twisted the cap off, we jingled our two bottles together: "Cheers." We laughed and quickly pressed the cool drinks to our lips: heads back, bottles extended toward the sky.

By the time we finished the Cokes, the small row of stores disappeared behind us. We passed the McCarthy house. All the McCarthy girls were redheads and not interested in Bobby or me.

We walked beyond the real estate office and came upon some road construction. New stainless-steel railings were being added to the small bridge that crossed the only stream on that side of town.

The rails were thick, hollow tubes attached to the cross-pieces holding the structure together. They were open at both ends.

Bobby ran ahead and asked me to look down one end, while he looked down the other.

"Hey, can you hear me?" Bobby whispered as I pressed my face into my end of the tube.

"What?" I called back.

Then, with his full strength, Bobby screamed, *"Can you hear me?"* Then he roared with laughter as I popped my head up out of the tube.

"Hey, that was a rotten trick."

Bobby grinned.

I walked along the bridge, patting my hand upon the smooth top of the rail until I reached Bobby, leaning against a telephone pole.

"Let's mail the bottles," he suggested.

"What?"

He took his bottle and pressed it into the open end of the rail. I did too.

The next day the construction workers closed the ends of the rails with heavy metal caps.

For many years, whenever I walked along that bridge, I'd give our rail a quick jab and listen to the two soda bottles jingle together.

Little Gods
and
Elephants

I was sitting in the dining room with my mother. Perhaps the noon meal was just finished. Perhaps there were snapdragons in the blue vase at the center of the table. I was a child, and my mother was describing to me the seven gods of luck.

My grandfather traveled through China in the early 1900s and collected wine vases, paintings, glass fish—small artifacts of an ancient world.

A two-inch Chinese carving sat deep inside the dining room cupboard. My mother pushed back the glass front, reached up to the top shelf, and lifted the small statue in her right hand.

"Do you see, Christopher, the seven little people surrounding the tree?" she asked as she sat close beside me.

I am sure my mother described all the people carved into the yellow ivory, but I remember just one: Fukurokuju. He was the old one with a high forehead, who was the symbol of fortune and longevity. His name made me laugh: Fukurokuju.

Children like the sounds of words and the incomplete stories of mythical beings. I did anyway. Perhaps this little god would hop into my pocket when I left for school and hide in my desk and help me with the multiplication tables. Fukurokuju.

I also remember being in my mother's bedroom, which was full of her books and held her desk and typewriter. The walls were covered with photographs of our family and friends.

"Open your hand and close your eyes, Christopher," my mother whispered. I remember closing my eyes and hearing her open a drawer, close a drawer. Then I felt the slightest tickle in the center of my open palm.

"Open your eyes."

I did and saw a small red pea with a small wood cork the size of a pencil point sticking up at one end.

"Pull out the little cap, Christopher, and turn the pea upside down."

With my giant fingers I held the pea in one hand, pulled out the stopper, turned the red pea over, and saw a small, small white object drop into my hand. It was the size of the tip of a butterfly's wing.

"Look closely," my mother said.

I leaned over my hand. The white speck in my hand was flat, with jagged edges. "An elephant! It's an elephant! The smallest elephant I've ever seen, and hidden inside the pea!"

I still do not know how the animal figure was cut to that size, and I do not wish to know. Elephants can live inside red peas. That's enough for children and for me.

How is it that children have such powers to dream? And such fears? When I was a small boy, I overheard someone speaking about a "diesel truck." In my mind I came to understand that the diesel truck was the largest, most powerful machine man had ever created, something to respect and to stand clear of whenever it passed through the neighborhood.

I sat on the front lawn for days, waiting to see this monster roar down the street. I expected something the size of the balloons at the Thanksgiving Day parade in New York City. I never saw my diesel truck, but for years, whenever I was on my bicycle and could see a truck approaching from either direction, I'd jump off the saddle, hold the handlebars tight, and wait for the roaring machine to pass.

We were all children once, accumulating bits of misinformation and scraps of fancy conjured up by a mother or a grandmother.

Yesterday Michael was busy in the side porch. I looked inside the sun-filled room and saw him painting a paper plate.

"That's very good, Michael."

"Don't look yet. I'm making something."

Thirty minutes later, while Roe and I were reading, and David and Karen were playing cards, Michael stepped into the living room. He had the multicolored paper plate tied flat upon his head, and he was waving a round blue fan with a hole in the middle toward his face. He announced, "I'm a Chinese boy, keeping cool." I have no idea where Michael came up with this idea, but there he was waving his fan and taking all sorts of important bows toward us.

What magic pole or rabbit hole need we follow in order to rediscover those little gods and elephants? Poets know the way, as do mothers and seven-year-old boys with their Chinese hats and blue fans. The question is, are you willing to follow them?

An

Evening's

Challenge

"Chris."

It was past midnight.

"Chris. There's a noise in the hall."

I was asleep.

"Chris. It sounds like something flying."

I heard the words "something flying" and rolled over, expecting to find Roe sleeping and me waking from a dream; instead I saw Roe sitting up in the darkness of our room.

"Chris, I hear this flapping sound."

"I'll go see." It is my job to go see.

As I twisted out from under the covers, I felt the cool air around my legs. I walked around the bed, past the rocking chair, past the closet, reached for the doorknob, and pulled. I was about to step into the hallway, when a dark flash zoomed past me, looped down within inches of my head, and dove into the darkness of David's room.

"Roe, you're right," I whispered. "There is something out here."

David was asleep under his dinosaur bedspread. Nothing wakes him. I pressed a switch. The light from the ceiling hurt my eyes. Just as I squinted, there was a sudden blur, flying, dancing, weaving back and forth like a drunken paddleball.

"Hey! It's a bat, Roe!"

"Do something," she called from our bedroom.

All I could do was duck. Perhaps I was a target. Husbands and fathers make good targets.

As I ducked, the bat zigzagged into the hall and into Michael's room. Roe poked her head out of our room. "He went that way."

"Well, why don't you go get him?" I was tempted to ask, but in the fine print of any wedding contract it clearly states: "Husband gets the bat."

I ran into Michael's room and leaned over his bed, picked him up to save him from the wild, little-boy-eating bat. Michael woke up halfway across the room. Ask children to get up for school and you would think their eyes were held together with a slow-dissolving glue, but if you release a bat in their room, instant life! "Daddy! What's that flying thing?" I tried to pretend that he was seeing things as I brought him into our bedroom, where I began tucking him under the covers. I walked back to Michael's room. The bat was still careening one way, then the other, with great speed.

I fell to my hands and knees in my underwear and began crawling toward the closed window. I could hear the movement of the air as the bat's wings flapped rapidly up and down. I could also hear Roe and Michael laughing in the next room.

I had read an article on bats in *The New Yorker* magazine a few weeks before. "They are gentle animals," I was told. I admire the magazine, the slick, smooth pages, the dark typeface and the quality of the writing, but I had a different perspective as I crawled back on my belly from the now open window after midnight while the bat circled around and around six inches from my head.

"Hey, Dad! That's neat!" Michael stuck his head into his room.

"He wanted to see the bat." Roe laughed. At times there is no dignity in being a father.

I pulled myself across the floor, slid into the hallway, and closed the door behind me.

"Maybe it will fly out the window."

Roe, Michael, and I walked back to our bedroom. "I want to be a bat for Halloween!" Michael whispered as we all tried to sleep.

After ten minutes, I began to think that I had to know for sure if the bat was gone. I once again slid out of bed and walked into the hallway, and slowly I opened Michael's bedroom door. Silence. No bat. But had it flown out of the house?

I jiggled Michael's bedcovers. Nothing. I stirred the toys in his toy chest. Nothing. I began slowly to pull the books from his bookshelf. Nothing. I tipped his entire bookshelf over onto the floor. Nothing. I went back to bed.

After another ten minutes, there was a small, delicate scratching. I ran back into Michael's room. On the far wall there hung a single picture: Beatrix Potter's Peter Rabbit in his blue suit. I pressed my cheek against the wall and checked behind the picture. If bats could grin, that bat would have grinned out at me then.

I ran out of the room, down the two flights of stairs to the basement, pulled the picnic cooler from its cardboard box, lifted the box over my head, and ran back up the two flights of stairs. Michael was waiting for me. He *did* wear a grin.

In his room, I placed the open side of the box over the entire picture against the wall. Then I ripped the curtain from the window, pulled the curtain rod out with my teeth, and used it to slide up the side of the wall to wiggle and unhook Peter Rabbit and the bat. *Thunk.* The picture frame and the freeloader plunked down inside the box.

"Roe. Can you find a large piece of cardboard?" She quickly returned with an unframed poster print of a girl and geese, which was affixed to a large, firm piece of cardboard. I slid the goose girl against the wall and over the open box, and presto, bat and Peter and Roe and Michael and Chris were all where I wanted them to be.

As I carried the large box before me, Roe moved furniture, kept Michael from tripping me, and opened the front door.

I stepped out into the darkness, slowly pulled off the goose girl print, and watched the bat in slow motion press its wings against the sudden freedom and disappear between the branches of the maple tree.

I took a bow in my white underwear, stepped into the house, lifted Michael into my arms, held Roe's hand, as the three of us climbed the stairs toward the liberated bedrooms.

And they say men can't be real men any longer in our society.

Cathy O'Shay

By October of my third year in grammar school, I was convinced that Cathy O'Shay was in love with me. As we stood in line for our coats one afternoon, she said, "Hi, Chris." She knew my name.

Cathy O'Shay had freckles, blue eyes, and short, curled brown hair cut in the fashion of 1960.

I didn't know she was beautiful, but I somehow knew that there was more to Cathy than tree forts, shooting off firecrackers, or eating marmalade sandwiches—which, for some reason, my older brother thought was the right thing to eat.

Sometime in November, I went food shopping with my mother and father. I know it was a Friday afternoon, because my parents always went food shopping on Friday afternoon at the same supermarket, Grandway, where televisions, mops, bananas, ironing boards, Ovaltine, and lobster could all be bought in a single afternoon under the same roof.

Shopping in Grandway was like going on an Australian walkabout: Pick out a cart with straight wheels. Walk past the pyramid of Schaefer beer. Greet Mr. Santini at the fruit-and-vegetable aisle. Haggle on a price for the bruised bananas and extra-ripe grapes Mr. Santini kept aside for my father. Beg my mother to let me push the cart and I won't zoom down the aisle and ride piggyback like I did last month, crashing into the Bosco chocolate syrup display.

Between hunting for the right can of tuna (the one with the fish who wore sunglasses while relaxing in a hammock) and weighing out the chestnuts my mother bought that week, my father treated me to an ice cream sundae over at the snack bar, just beyond the cereal aisle. We men both liked chocolate with an extra scoop of sprinkles spread generously over the top of the dish.

After we finished eating, I spun around on the stool a few times until I was dizzy, then I jumped off, following my father as he began looking for my mother.

Still a bit wobbly from my spin on the stool, I pretended I was Superman walking on top of a blimp and any minute the blimp would explode killing all aboard unless I was able to secure the patch over the gaping hole just out of my reach. I was about to make a dramatic lunge, when I saw, down the cereal aisle, Cathy O'Shay with her mother and father. She waved. I waved. She turned the corner and disappeared, and then the blimp exploded.

I had a secret.

"Chris, wipe the chocolate sprinkles from the corner of your mouth," my father said as he spotted my mother picking up a *TV Guide*.

In mid-December, Mrs. Buttress, the third-grade teacher, announced our Christmas party. "We all have to bring something in. Raise your hand when I go down the list. Paper plates? Amanda. Napkins? Joe." There were sixty-three children in our class that year. I volunteered to bring in a bag of potato chips.

On the day of the party, we all carried our contributions into the classroom.

"Everyone settle down," Mrs. Buttress said as she began giving napkins to everyone. "Each person who has something please walk around the classroom and hand out what you brought."

One girl distributed cups. A boy counted five M&M's per person. I walked around and let everyone grab a handful of chips from my bag.

We were nearly ready to begin the party. I was already sitting when the door to our room opened and in stepped Cathy O'Shay, carrying a tray. Sitting on the tray were twenty-five marshmallow Santa Claus treats. Each was identical to each: the bodies were made with two large, fat marshmallows held together with toothpicks. The arms and heads were smaller marshmallows, also kept in place with toothpicks. Sitting on the top of each white Santa Claus was a small red paper hat rolled from thick paper, and at the tip of each hat, the smallest marshmallow.

I wanted a marshmallow Santa Claus.

Cathy began handing out her offering, beginning at the row closest to the door. Obviously she didn't have enough for the entire class. Up and down the rows she went, lifting a Santa Claus and placing it on the desk of this friend and that.

By the time she reached the fourth row, she had ten Santas left. Eight. Six. Cathy turned up the sixth row. Five left. Three. She then began walking down my row, the one beside the window. Cathy picked up the second to the last Santa Claus and handed it to Mark, then she slowly lifted up the last one, the last white marshmallow Santa Claus that she, Cathy O'Shay, had made with her own hands. She looked to her right. She took a few steps. She turned toward me. "Remember, I saved you from the exploding blimp," I wanted to shout. Cathy lifted Santa and placed him gently on my desk. She smiled and licked her fingers.

"Let's sing 'Joy to the World' before we eat," Mrs. Buttress suggested. I am sure I sang the loudest that December morning thirty-four years ago.

After the song, as everyone began eating, I quickly took my marshmallow Santa Claus, wrapped him in my napkin, and stashed him in my book bag.

In the bus on the way home, I took Santa out of the bag and held him in my cupped hands as if he were both Tinker Bell and Kryptonite—something delicate and capable of joining me on any adventure, yet full of enough power to kill anyone—my sister, say —who discovered what I had and why I was keeping it.

Mercifully my sister was out ice-skating with a friend when I got home. My mother thought I had made the marshmallow Santa as some sort of school project. "Hang up your coat. There's a Christmas card on your dresser from your grandmother. Your father will be home early tonight."

I ran up the stairs, stepped into my room, and closed the door behind me. After I read my grandmother's card and stuffed the five dollars in my pocket, I placed my marshmallow Santa Claus on the top of my dresser, in the very middle, just below the mirror. He sat there like a Buddha.

Do you know what happens to marshmallows if they sit in the open for several months? They begin to shrink, wrinkle, dry up like prunes.

One day after school, as I stepped into the house, my mother said, "Chris, I did some heavy cleaning in your room today." That is all she had to say. I flew up the stairs with invisible speed. My mother had tossed out the dried marshmallows, but she left on the dresser the small red paper hat Cathy had rolled between her fingertips back when Clark Kent was just a cub reporter.

Well, DC Comics just killed off Superman, but my mother expects me home for my forty-third Christmas this year, and I still remember a nine-year-old boy who once had a secret that was greater than marmalade and firecrackers.

Songs
of
Sexuality

CANTO IV

My nobler self, detached from language and earth,
A demigod prepared to drape my window
With curtains of grief and bay leaves
Torn from the garden,

Feels the heat from the lamp at my desk
In blue-and-white darkness.

Tonight I refine my single purpose
To turn away from what is ordinary:
A desire to be caressed as would a child
In the afternoon as the water boils on the stove
And steam rises to the ceiling:
Hot shapes and white curls.

I drink my tea as the children sleep
And my wife is reading
While the stars retain their positions
And I burn in the rage of this royal flight
Back and forth between what is felt
And what is necessary—
Not like the stars, which are not necessary
And worn upon the heads of college girls
As they pass before my open window
In the darkness after a free day at Langsworth Field.

Sparkle
and
Bang

It is difficult to do what is right when we are confronted with temptation.

When I was eleven, my best friend, Johnny, and I rode our bicycles downtown, with quarters in our pockets and with a plan: We were going to buy Sparkle and Bang matches.

I have never seen these matches again since those days in the early sixties. They were what looked like ordinary books of paper matches. Printed on the cover of the Sparkle variety was the image of red shooting stars zooming across the sky. The Bang matches sported a design of a cannon that had just exploded.

They were wonderful. If you struck a Sparkle match, a burst of white lights and a quick flame shot out before you, like magic. The match would sizzle, quickly turn to smoke, and extinguish itself in your hand.

The Bang matches were more threatening. After you struck a Bang match, you had to quickly toss it to the ground, where it gave off a small, sharp snap, like a powerful cap.

Johnny and I rode our bikes home, ran through the woods, through his uncle's field, and to the hidden pond.

This pond was in the northwest corner of the pepper field, completely concealed by mock-orange bushes. This is where Johnny and I shot off our matches.

Of course it was forbidden. Of course we could have set the neighborhood on fire, and of course it was better than school and sisters and swimming lessons, as we sat at the edge of the pond in the darkness of our "cave," striking one match after another, watching the glow of the Sparkles reflect in each other's faces, and tossing the Bang matches at each other's feet with a snicker.

No one ever knew that Johnny and I spent that forbidden afternoon together.

Last July 4, Roe and I and the children, as well as a number of other friends and their children, spent the day at our local beach. Hamburgers were eaten. Horseshoes clanged. The day splashed on. We closed the park late that afternoon.

After everyone drove home, after Roe and I unpacked the car, as the children were climbing the back steps into the house, David shouted, "I left my mitt at the beach!"

Roe looked at me. I looked at David. "I'll go back and see if I can find it."

As I rolled the car down the driveway, Karen waved out the dining room window. I waved too.

The park was just a few minutes across town, past Jones' Hardware store, past the First Reformed Church, left at the light, and beyond the railroad tracks.

I walked along the fence of the closed beach, trying to see through the grove of trees where we had eaten our picnic dinner. No luck.

As I turned back toward the car, I noticed, at the far end of the parking lot, a large green garbage Dumpster. I do not know why I thought that the mitt might have been dumped there by the lifeguards. I knew they cleaned the beach at the end of each day. I knew there was a lost and found. But I thought I'd check the Dumpster anyway. Perhaps I felt it would give me a sense that I had tried all avenues to find what I was looking for.

I drove to the edge of the empty parking lot, stopped the car, and lifted the heavy Dumpster lid, which fell back with a loud crash of metal on metal.

As I stood in the shadow of the five-foot-high waste receptacle, I looked to my left, to my right. I hoisted myself up, and then I jumped down into the dark cavern. The sound of my heavy descent echoed like a bass drum. The deep Dumpster was empty except for a single thick pornographic magazine.

I heard someone say once that integrity is doing the right thing when no one is watching. Well, I sat down in the middle of the empty trash bin, cross-legged, and turned carefully each page of that magazine, cover to cover.

I never saw such a thing. The men were muscular; the women sleek and firm. There was surely a sparkle and a bang in the photographs, but like those matches, after the initial flash, all that was left was smoke, darkness, and then a foul smell, or was it the lingering odor of the Dumpster?

Sparkle and Bang matches temporarily filled the void of a boring afternoon for two boys crawling out from under the mock-orange bushes, and pornography temporarily fills the void in the hearts of sad, lonely people longing to be embraced.

Both activities can lead to a fire that destroys what is natural, beautiful, and good.

Beauty

Versus

Ugliness

The first time I saw a nude woman I was a graduate student at Columbia University, on my way back from one of my English classes. It was in the spring of 1974. I was twenty-three years old.

I just left the class where we had been discussing "The Love Song of J. Alfred Prufrock," by T. S. Eliot: "I have heard the mermaids singing, each to each."

I walked down the front steps of Philosophy Hall and noticed a large collection of people at the center of the campus. The grass was green again; the leaves were soft and new. The crowd was surprisingly silent.

As I walked closer and closer, I saw with clarity what was at the center of the crowd: A nude young woman was sprawled out upon the stone arms of the Alma Mater. The young woman's clothes were folded neatly at the base of the statue. I didn't know why she was there. I didn't understand if there was a political message in her gesture. I was, however, startled with the woman's beauty.

The first time I was so dazzled with the human form of a woman was at the Metropolitan Museum of Art. I encountered a marble sculpture of a nude woman who was in a standing position: her right leg slightly bent at the knee, her head turned to one side. Could marble possibly be so soft? I asked myself.

On that spring afternoon of long ago, a bald man with glasses standing next to me in the crowd, a stranger, turned, curved his lips into a deep, wide smile, raised his eyebrows, and laughed, implying that he and I were engaged in some loose, crass, free moment of pure entertainment and cheap thrills as we watched the girl brush her hair away from her face while she sat in the soft shadow of the college's symbolic mother. That is when I walked away, carrying my books under my limp arms.

In Eliot's poem there is an echo: "I grow old . . . I grow old . . . " I often tell my high school students that they will have to figure things out for themselves: love, sex, careers, loneliness.

My son Michael said recently at the dinner table that there was a boy in his class who told a bad thing about body parts. I inform my children that there will always be people in their world who will try and make beautiful things ugly: music, art, nature, the human form.

For three years, I tutored a boy with muscular dystrophy. His legs and arms were as thin as bones. His feet were twisted. He couldn't walk. His rib cage protruded through his shirt. After an afternoon lesson on John Steinbeck's novel *The Grapes of Wrath*, the boy invited me to stay because he had hired a woman to perform a striptease for him and some of his friends that evening. I declined the invitation and drove home. It was raining that night. I remember wiping my hands against the cold windshield, trying to clear away the condensation that was collecting there. The glass was smooth and wet. I like the sound of wiper blades clicking back and forth.

Between the marble goddess in the museum and the striptease, between the nude young woman sitting on the statue and the man in the crowd who snickered, there exists a clear division: beauty that is beautiful and beauty that is ugly.

A beautiful woman is a woman with a name, a history, a voice we recognize, stories, pictures, laughs, combs and brushes on the dresser. An ugly woman has no name.

Lust is the smooth, cold, wet windshield under our stiff hands in the dark. Love is one human being standing beside another, exchanging mutual gifts of our bodies, songs, dreams—perhaps madness, but in such madness we return to the next morning whole and complete, until the emptiness begins to return and we seek once again what is beautiful or what is ugly. Both will fill up the void, but only one will keep us alive.

Beauty
and
the Beast

We were given a trust in the first days of creation. I call it the trust of our being: female and male, divided parts to nurture, develop, and share.

Only in our joining together can we discover our whole being once again.

More and more, it seems, we are stepping away from our original trust of what it means to be a man and to be a woman. Isn't anyone tired of the false images that we are beating ourselves with day after day, images in the newspaper, in movies, and on television, images of lost women hooked to shades of lipstick and re-shaped bodies, hoping to fit into new forms that were never intended to blend with the grasslands? Does anyone want to laugh at the images of men slouching back into the caves, pounding on drums, beating their breasts, offering up their anxiety to an unknown god usually called stress? I call it a fear of death.

One spring, when my daughter was four years old, I was sitting on the grass with my brother and sister. Jose was on a blue lawn chair, reading a book of poetry by Wendell Berry, one of our greatest living American poets.

My sister Maria and I were talking about some graphic designs for a theater company playbill she was working on.

As we talked, little Karen walked along the new blades of

grass. She turned to my right and approached a wall of green ivy. She reached before her, turned her fingers around a single ivy leaf, and pulled until the leaf snapped from its vine. Jose, behind his book, did not notice that Karen was walking toward him, the leaf in her hand.

Maria and I stopped talking as we watched Karen slowly step up to my brother.

Karen stopped and stood before Jose, before the open book, then she simply lifted her right arm, dropped the single leaf onto Jose's lap, and said, with great authority, "Now you are a toad."

Jose picked right up on the game. He slid under his book and wiggled off his chair, as Karen backed away and began to laugh. Then Jose crouched into a toad position and gave out a loud, powerful toad sound and jumped forward in the direction of a little girl in a yellow dress and black shoes.

"Croak! Croak! Croak! Arrrgh!"

That is when Karen began to run and cry all the way up the stone steps from the garden and into the house.

Karen discovered, at the age of four, the power women possess to turn their men into beasts. She also had the power to turn the beast into a prince, but she was not going to give it a try that afternoon.

We are all given a single leaf, a talisman, this trust that holds within its veins the power to transform those we love into soothed, peaceful people in need of constant reminders that we are here to exchange our gentle parts with each other.

Sex

In the novel *Narcissus and Goldmund*, Hermann Hesse makes distinctions between desire and love.

I was groping for a way to make this idea clear to my high school students during our discussion of the first eighty pages of the book. What personal example of peaceful sexuality could I offer my students, who believe that sex is for recreation, for salvation, is a cure for loneliness or a goal to conquer. I came up with an answer that evening while Roe attended a parent/school meeting and I was home with the children.

"Karen? Why don't you get your book, and I'll read a bit before you go to bed."

"OK, Daddy," Karen quickly agreed, pulling out her favorite book of the moment from her schoolbag: *Pippi Longstocking*, by Astrid Lindgren.

Karen curled her body into the letter *C* and cuddled against my side on the couch.

I began to read where I had left off the day before, where Pippi and her friends were sitting on a fence.

Karen and I began to drift into the world of Villa Villekulla, when we heard Michael laughing. We both looked up. There he was, wedged within the doorframe of the kitchen, with his head nearly touching the ceiling. Michael likes to press his hands and feet against opposite sides of the frame and wiggle up like a monkey between two trees.

Again Karen and I returned to the novel. Michael was still laughing and giggling in the kitchen. Suddenly I heard a loud scratching on the back door. Mittens, our cat, has learned that if she clings to the screen door and climbs up the entire length, she can lean over the window curtains and cry to be let in.

The cat was meowing and scratching; Michael was giggling and crashing to the floor; I was trying to read about Pippi. That is when David decided to begin his fifteen-minute trumpet practice upstairs in his room. What a racket!

This is what sexuality is all about.

We cannot escape our loneliness by throwing ourself into the bodies of those we desire. We cannot cling to the false sense of ecstasy that we feel during orgasm. Sexual desire ought not be the center of our dreams, the path to consolation. That is love's domain.

Love is the consequence of our deep commitment to the possibilities in others. Love is creation, trusting the future, the embracing of another human being in the belief that this embace will produce something new and good. Desire ends in satisfaction. Love begins in commitment, leads to making love, and grows in the sounds of children laughing in the kitchen, blowing into a trumpet, giggling next to a father. That is what sex is all about.

Love
and
Sex

After teaching in high schools for sixteen years, I have come to believe that we are not offering young people a sufficient explanation of what it means to be sexual beings. The motion picture industry, the television industry, the advertising community, have all given teenagers images of sexuality that are connected to automobiles, beer, money, lust, greed. Where is the poetry? Where is the innocence?

Schools across the country are delivering information to young people on sexuality, intercourse, the reproductive system, diseases, contraceptives. They are given statistics, biology, charts, facts. Are they given images of love? Concepts of loneliness? Explanations of courage? Statistics on forgiveness? Discussions about living in a community?

In seventh grade, I knew a boy, Jack. He was the type of person who made a grand entrance on the playground each morning. He was never satisfied with simply coasting upon the blacktop and steering his bike cautiously toward the bicycle rack. Instead he would give a loud whoop as he rounded the edge of the woods and charge onto the playground. Jack would pedal as hard as he could, and seconds before crashing into our bicycles in the rack, he'd jam his foot down upon the brake, lock his rear wheel, twist the bicycle around with a squeal of rubber, and then give another shout.

Jack had arrived. He'd step off his bicycle, pick it up over his head, and heave it on top of the other bikes, neatly lined up in their places.

I saw Jack break a boy's nose in a fight, throw his own lunch against the cafeteria wall. I saw him take a swing at the principal, and I saw him walk up the halls between classes and quickly fondle a girl's breasts as he passed her.

I did not want to be like Jack, but I, too, was interested in Sara, the particular girl he attacked one morning. I liked her dark hair and the way she laughed. I wanted to love her. Sara was the first girl I held in my arms. Remember the last twenty minutes of your eighth-grade dance?

Something was at work inside me, something undeveloped, but real and wonderful. This was an early hint of a future existence. How we respond to this hint helps to determine the type of people we will someday be.

Jack bullied his desires on the girl. Is that how to embrace what is beautiful? I knew there was something beyond desire and grabbing. I felt there was something good and innocent and mysterious about my feelings toward this girl, but I didn't understand it exactly.

A father in his forties recently told me that he was sexually active in high school but he had established a few ground rules, which he passed on to his teenage sons: "Rule number one: Don't get the girl pregnant. Rule number two: Use protection. And rule number three: Don't let those people who would disapprove know what you are doing. That way," the father told me, "my sons aren't hurting anyone."

There is no doubt that the "civilized" world has placed difficult constraints upon adolescents. There have been many cultures in which young people are considered adults at the onset of puberty. In such societies, teenagers become sexually active, responding to their normal, powerful, and wonderful physical desires.

But where does this leave our teenagers? Young people enter puberty and come to experience a new longing for a caress, but we do not accept them as adults, do not accept the notions of teenagers making love; we deny them clear, jubilant, honest access to their sexuality until they are married. Don't. Don't. Don't. That is about all the advice we adults give adolescents today.

Young people want to know what they can do about these real and exciting and new feelings, but too often there isn't anyone to give them answers. So they seek wisdom from television, movies, and commercials. I believe many young people are sent away from these images with false answers, answers that are not appropriate to their own questions.

Young people discover a longing to bring a physical presence close to their hearts and bodies. We human beings are built for this. At a very early age, we begin to suspect that we are made up of broken parts, and we try to join with others to make ourselves whole and complete.

Teenagers quickly discover that human beings seek to fill the loneliness of ourselves with the loneliness of others and thereby discover hints of peace.

During that year of my eighth grade, someone wrote "Chris and Sara" in bright red paint on the wall of the train underpass. A few days later, I painted a red heart around the two names. We became friends, Sara and I. We danced together in high school, exchanged letters in college, went our separate ways, lost contact.

After completing my writing for the evening, I walk up from the basement, turn off the single light Roe has left for me in the living room. I climb the stairs. To my left is seven-year-old Michael's room, where he can be found sleeping under his covers or on top of a wild collection of stuffed animals and books he accumulated on his bed. One night, I found that he had crawled into his pillowcase, the pillow still inside, and was happily asleep, curled up like a chicken in an egg, as he informed me the next morning.

To the left of Michael's room, my nine-year-old daughter sleeps. Each night I admire Karen's closed eyes. I listen to her breathing. She sleeps with her socks on.

David's room is just beyond the linen closet. He is twelve. His curtains and bedspread are covered with bright-colored dinosaurs: red ones, green ones, blue ones. When he was four, David announced that he wanted to be a paleontologist.

I kiss all the children as they sleep, and I often place my hand on their heads and bless them. Is it all right for a father to repeat a holy blessing above his children in the darkness?

And then I step into the room where Roe, too, is sleeping. When we go to bed at the same time, I give her a back rub, or we make love, or we talk, or we do all three in one order or another.

When I am finished writing for the night and the lights in the neighborhood are extinguished and I climb those narrow steps, after I kiss the children, after I slip into bed beside Roe, I often look through the faint light and darkness about our room and I feel like the loneliest man in the world, until my wife stirs or my son coughs in the darkness, and then I sleep.

I, too, will have rules about sexuality when my children become teenagers:

Rule number one: Learn who you are.

Rule number two: Try as best you can to be patient.

Rule number three: Understand that you will never escape that small feeling of loneliness.

Rule number four: Understand that someone is out there waiting to fall in love with you.

Rule number five: Understand that you will find this person and be in love too.

Rule number six: Date as many people as you can.

Rule number seven: Understand that you are the only one who has to figure out how to handle your own sexuality.

Rule number eight: Understand that there are people who will try to turn everything that is beautiful into something ugly, including sex and the human body.

Rule number nine: Make love to the person you fall in love with.

Rule number ten: If you do not know who you are, you cannot possibly abide by rule number nine.

Rule number eleven: Remember that when your great-grandfather died, your great-grandmother clipped a lock of his hair and kept it in a small pouch around her neck, and she sang church songs all alone at night in her living room for ten years until she, too, died, a happy woman.

Songs
of
Old Age

CANTO V

It is ten o'clock, after a few pages of MacLeish
The biography, a noticed time to write poetry.
I bring, perhaps, the image of daisies on the kitchen shelf,
Anniversary flowers for a further keeping
Between my wife and me as we continue
Our constant understanding of love that is fantasy
Held in hand under the edge of her cotton nightgown.

Before I go down, under the floorboards,
Beyond the sight of the moon,
Into my basement room where the roots of grass
Do not reach, I feel for my shoes in the darkness.
It is my secret, my own doubt:
To create what could destroy a normal man,
Or to sleep without such creation and die
An uncommon death, which is to live without
A sense of giving back what has been given
In a single crack of birth split out upon
The world to make a new attempt at
The old desire: renewal of the failed waters,
A recasting of the mountains into a new mold
To behold a new ascent toward heaven
Or an attempt to reach the plateau.

We can barely see the outer edges of
A certain place we believe is heaven,
Or so I think when I walk down my stairs
And begin to write, against all odds:
Abandoned flowers, shoes upon my feet;
My lost hopes to become MacLeish.

Mrs. Webster

The eighth-grade lunch in the cafeteria when I was thirteen began with Mrs. Webster and her whistle. As we all rushed into the wide, open room and sprawled out on the cafeteria chairs, Mrs. Webster stepped to the center of our swirling bodies and loud voices, took a long inhale, and blew one single blast from a fat silver whistle that hung around her neck on a white cord tied in a crude knot.

"Today," Mrs. Webster would screech out, "we have sloppy joes, french fries, corn, and pears. The soup is chicken, the sandwiches are cheese, peanut butter, or cold cuts mixed."

Mrs. Webster always wore a white uniform, thick-heeled white shoes, glasses. Her hair was stacked into a crazy pile upon her head. She was short, had a curled lip, and controlled the wide universe with the power of her whistle and a nasty look on her face. I always connected her with noise, catcalls, hooting and laughing, plates bouncing on the floors, empty milk cartons stomped upon, which created a loud pop and a possible trip to the principal's office if Mrs. Webster caught you.

When I entered high school, I quickly forgot Mrs. Webster. Four years later, I was a lifeguard at the local public swimming pool. One June morning, the pool director tacked up an announcement about the first summer lecture: "Robins. One o'clock in the trees."

"The trees" was a small collection of maples beyond the pool's main gate, which provided plenty of shade and comfort for the children as they gathered around the guest lecturer.

The children at the pool asked me if I knew what the talk was going to be about. "Robins."

A few minutes before one o'clock, I blew my whistle to remind anyone interested that the lecture was about to begin. Some children took my hand, and together we proceeded to the trees. There, sitting on the bench, was old, old Mrs. Webster, beside a gold birdcage. The trees formed a near-perfect circle around her.

The children and I stepped in among the trees, and one by one we sat upon the dried grass around our visitor.

"Now," Mrs. Webster began, "robins make blue eggs." She leaned toward the gold cage, opened the doors, and reached in toward a bird, which sat on its perch.

"My cat brought home this robin. It didn't have feathers yet. Its eyes weren't open."

The bird jumped upon Mrs. Webster's finger, and she held it before us in the open air. The children jumped up all at once, anxious to hold the bird, pet its feathers.

"No. You'll have to sit," Mrs. Webster whispered. "You don't want to spook him."

The children sat down.

"Robins migrate. They hunt for bugs and worms. They will live in the same yard summer after summer . . ." And she sang on and on about the bird upon her finger, while the children and I and the summer all leaned toward the center of the trees, receiving the story of the robin.

"Now if you are careful, children, you can one by one come up and pet the bird before I place him back in his cage."

Our world is a confusing place. It is difficult, sometimes, to know what is really important, but every now and then look out across the dried grass and see the children under the circle of trees. Take a close look as an old woman holds up her robin beside the gold cage. Listen to the children laugh. Who should then say you haven't discovered the center of the universe?

Miss Bebe

Miss Bebe, a family friend, was always old. She came to visit my mother and father on an irregular basis. She drove a car and could just see above the steering wheel.

I remember watching her open the car door, turn her crooked body toward the steps of our porch. She grabbed the car window with her right hand and pushed herself out of the car with her left.

She often wore a wide purple straw hat.

"Christopher, if you'll just reach in on the back seat of my car, you'll find a bag."

As Miss Bebe twisted and creaked up the steps, into my mother's warm embrace, I followed with a large shopping bag in my arms.

All I remember about Miss Bebe is that she spent much of her time in a place called Rumson, New Jersey, which must be near the sea, for she always brought us a box of saltwater taffy with "Best Wishes from Rumson, N.J." printed on the side.

"Bring me the bag, Christopher." She always called me by my full name.

She reached into the wide bag and pulled out the box of taffy. Her hands reminded me of those carnival machines with a mechanical claw you can guide with levers, hoping to grasp a watch or a pink cow or a bracelet for your sister.

I remember sitting beside Miss Bebe on the living room couch.

The sagging cushions caused her to lean up against me as she pulled the clear wrapping off the box.

"I've brought you and your brothers and sisters some taffy from Rumson."

"Yes, Miss Bebe. Thank you."

She extended her crooked finger and pointed to a postcard glued to the lid of the box.

"Here is the ocean," she said, like a guide, as we converged on the billowing cushions. "And look at the girls and boys splashing in the water."

I could smell her perfume. She kept her hat on. The living room window was open as the hot summer air pressed against the torn screen.

Miss Bebe opened the box. "Take one."

I usually took a green piece. The shape of school chalk, the taffies were wrapped in wax paper, which was twisted at both ends like Tootsie Rolls.

"I'll take a pink one," Miss Bebe said.

I liked to pull on both sides of the paper, as if I were tying a shoe. The candy unrolled, then I found the seam of the paper, pulled out the taffy, and inserted the entire piece in my mouth. So did Miss Bebe.

We sat together in silence, cheek to cheek, chewing and chewing and chewing, until she turned to me, laughed, gave me a hug, and began talking to my parents about history or a new book, or about something less interesting than saltwater taffy.

Children belong to the ocean waves, to the distant memories glued upon a white candy box. I liked sharing the cushion with Miss Bebe.

Fill in the
Empty Spaces

During the horrible battle at Vicksburg in the Civil War, the two armies had reached a standstill. After days and days of the tense wait, a soldier from the North stood up from his trench. Suddenly a soldier from the South also stood up out of his trench. The two men looked at each other over the short distance between them. They both waited, until the fellow from the North shouted, "What'd you stand up for?"

"Because you did!" the soldier from the South shouted back. After they thought about this for a moment, they both returned to their fortifications and continued with the fight.

The smaller the distance between us human beings, the more we tend to be willing to trust each other.

About twice a year, Roe and I take the children to a county zoo. We look first at the alligators, then at the mountain lion. The children like to squawk in the aviary and scratch their sides as we pass the monkey cage.

At some point, we usually have ice cream from the ice cream truck—chocolate cones, Italian ice, sherbet on a stick—and we always ride the train.

What I like best about this ride is how the children sit to the right and left of Roe and me and, as we steam through the zoo, wave at everyone who is watching us, and the crowd waves back, strangers waving to us as if we were their lost relatives returning from a long voyage.

What is that space we try to fill between human beings? There is no better place for a person than to be in the arms of someone he or she loves. We do not embrace strangers, but we can smile, raise our hands in greeting. The hard part comes when we have to allow that space to widen between us and those we have grown to trust and love.

Each spring after my grandfather died, my grandmother would visit my mother and father, my sisters and brothers and me, arriving in a 747 nonstop from Brussels. She would come in April in her black coat, her feathered hat, and her white gloves.

Every night when we went to bed during those summers of long ago, my grandmother would step into our rooms, lean over us, and say, in Flemish, "A little cross and a sleep well," as she traced a small *X* on our smooth foreheads with her wrinkled thumb.

In October 1982, it was time, once again, to drive my grandmother back to Kennedy Airport in New York for her flight home. In the terminal, she pretended that she couldn't walk very well. She was ninety-two, but she could walk perfectly well; however, she knew that if she had a wheelchair, she didn't have to wait on line and she would be among the first taken onto the airplane. She always took great pleasure in acting out this role.

A ground agent for the airline greeted us at the main desk. My grandmother took her place in the wheelchair. On her lap she balanced her purse, a small cloth sack, and her coat. It was difficult to tell where she began and where her travel gear ended.

I remember walking along on my grandmother's left; my mother was on her right, and the airline agent pushed her forward.

We would not be seeing my grandmother until the following spring. Parting is never a sweet sorrow.

There was a thirty-minute wait until the passengers could board. The woman pushing the wheelchair said she'd be right back, and my mother and father, my grandmother and I, sat in the lounge. It is an odd thing that at such a sad moment we talked about the condition of the carpets and the color of the chairs.

Too soon the agent returned. "Time to say goodbye."

My mother and father kissed my grandmother, then, as I leaned over to do the same, she hugged me and whispered, "A little cross and a sleep well."

The ground agent pushed my grandmother past the check-in desk and down a small passageway toward two large doors. Just before she reached the doors, the woman turned the wheelchair around so that we could wave.

I will never forget watching my grandmother struggling under her bags and coat, trying to lift her white-gloved hand. My mother and father and I waved. The distance was growing wider and wider between us. Finally my grandmother was able to free her hand, and she waved too.

The wheelchair, the ground agent, and my grandmother disappeared behind the closed gray doors.

I never saw my grandmother again. She died that winter and was buried beside my grandfather.

The smaller the distance we keep between people, the better the chances are that we will be a little less frightened of each other, and a little less lonely.

I wish my grandmother were coming this spring.

Charlie

When I went to college, I kept up a correspondence with my parents, with a few friends from high school, and with Rosie, my childhood baby-sitter, who was, in my mind, my American grandmother.

My father's parents died before I was born. My mother's mother lived in Belgium. But Rosie was as close to a grandmother as anyone could expect. She remembered my birthday, had a house filled with grandmother smells of flowers and perfume, expected me to come and rake her leaves in the fall and dig out her sidewalk after a winter storm.

During my lonely college years, my correspondence was a link to what I loved and what I hoped someday to re-create for myself, which I never did. Times of youth cannot be lived again. Things will never be as bright or as tall or as dramatic as they were when a boy of eight watched the late afternoon's sun illuminate the tips of the summer maple trees.

But I did love Rosie, and although my days of sitting on her porch and listening to her tell stories about riding the trolleys in New York were gone, I could still write and tell her what she meant to me as a child and now as a young man lost in a world he was not yet prepared to understand.

After six months of correspondence, Rosie wrote to say how

much she enjoyed receiving letters, and did I know anyone in my dorm who might like to "pick up a correspondence with an old gal who could still type seventy-five words a minute?"

I didn't dare ask anyone on my floor if he would like to send Rosie letters. Most people in my dorm were interested in either the next basketball game or the next drink. So I invented Charlie.

What harm could it do, I thought, if Rosie received a letter from a new friend now and again, which I could easily create.

I always corresponded in longhand, so I had "Charlie" type his letters to Rosie. Charlie was bright, full of energy. He knew how to dazzle the girls; he enjoyed long walks through the Allegheny Mountains, drove a jeep, and sang baritone in a barbershop quartet. Every two weeks, Charlie wrote Rosie a letter.

She loved him, thought he had a terrific sense of humor, was flattered that he took such an interest in her African violet collection.

During my Easter vacation, when I visited Rosie, she said she hoped that Charlie would be able to come and see her over the summer. I told her Charlie lived in Hawaii.

I was caught up in a lie that I thought was simply an innocent way to please a lonely old woman.

After two years, I had developed a long, involved relationship between Charlie and Rosie. I had to keep notes, reminding myself that Charlie had two sisters, a mother who worked in a chemical lab, and a father who hated television and played the organ. Charlie sent Rosie birthday cards and a box of chocolates on Christmas, and he told her about this girl he loved.

I'd have Charlie ask eighty-year-old Rosie about her life, and she'd send back long, wonderful letters describing Sunday picnics, Pete the parrot, who had sat on the trolley conductor's shoulder, and how she used to win all the pinochle games over at the firehouse.

I made the mistake of saying that Charlie loved pinochle, so I had to learn all the rules of the game so Charlie could have a good laugh over a few of his most famous games. Rosie laughed too.

Finally I transferred out of my first college. Rosie became ill. During one of my last visits before she died, she asked me what had ever happened to that nice young man.

"He joined the army, Rosie, then I lost track of him."

Rosie liked that. Her son was a former marine.

"When you see Charlie someday, tell him I love him very much."

I took Rosie's old hand and pressed it against my cheek. "He loves you very much too."

Songs
of
Death

CANTO VI

I bring to my grave a collection of stones
Gathered from the garden of my first home,
Where my father planted roses.

I bring the stones of my second home,
Where my wife gathered daffodils
The size of stars and just as bright.

I have with me the stones of my children,
Born under the belly of the receding glacier,
Left upon wet soil for my taking.

I bring the stones of my poetry,
Little pebbles worn smooth from worry.

Take what I have collected,
Scatter them one by one
On the fresh-turned soil over my grave,
Return the stones to disorder; let them lie
And wait for some new boy to discover them
Along the way; let him place each in a sack
For his own distant sowing.

In Memoriam

The obituary sections of our newspapers across the country have something in common: If you are famous, you earn a long eulogy in newsprint, listing all your accomplishments, important dates, awards received, degrees earned. If you are lucky, there will be a photograph, taken when you were thirty or forty.

If you are not a famous person, you will be given a single sentence, perhaps a paragraph, if you receive any space at all.

Even in our dying we attach labels to each other, trying to make distinctions.

Here is a partial list of people I have known who have died without causing many people to take notice:

Ruth: Died in her late fifties of cancer . . . devoted her life to teaching. Her favorite color was purple. Her voice on the phone following her first operation sounded like a machine, but I recognized her laugh. Her husband died after eight years of marriage, and her only son was severely retarded. I liked the smell of her perfume.

Jeanne: Seventeen years old . . . one of my first students. She died in a car accident on the way to school in a dense morning fog. Her cheeks were round. She liked to tease the teachers in the hallway. I remember how white her shoes were as she danced in the school production of *The Music Man.* She was Marian the librarian.

Charles: He was my uncle. I never met him. I knew he liked chocolate, was a missionary in the order of the White Fathers of Africa, painted birds, and dropped dead in a Paris street while mailing a letter to my aunt.

Mrs. Jones: A neighbor when I was a child. She died in her nineties. For years her house remained empty and unsold. My sister Anne and I crossed the street each summer, climbed Mrs. Jones's cherry tree, and helped ourselves until we looked like clowns with wide red lips. One afternoon, Mrs. Jones invited my mother for tea. She took my mother upstairs, opened the top drawer of a bedroom dresser. It contained beautiful folded white baby clothes: a shirt, small socks, a hat, and a dress. Mrs. Jones never had any children.

Bob: He was a college professor who liked to create puns, read, collect classical records. He knew the names of most art museums in the world and what each held. He loved his niece, taught teachers how to teach literature to high school students. Bob treated Roe and me to a dinner in Paris on our honeymoon.

Baba: My grandmother. She died in her nineties. She lived alone in Brussels, sang church songs aloud to herself in the middle of winter. The last summer she came to America for a visit, I took her to a carnival. In the distance we heard the music of the carousel. "I'd like to ride the horse," she said. I held her arm as she stepped up onto the platform. I had to lift her on the wooden horse, which grinned. As the carousel music began, the horse began to bob up and down, which startled my grandmother, then she laughed and laughed as the carousel spun around.

Chuck: A car salesman most of his life. He had a big nose, wore suspenders, took great pride in his tulips and his Christmas decorations. He was an auxiliary policeman who liked to direct traffic where there wasn't much need for direction, but he waved to my children in the back seat and brought gingerbread cookies his wife made and was too polite to step into the house, no matter how cold it was outside.

Peggy: I don't know much about Peggy. She had white hair, was a Republican, spoke French, loved her husband. Some of her children lived in London. Peggy had a house in the next development, through the trees and around the corner. The children liked to ring her doorbell on Halloween. In the fall, there was always a small table at the end of the driveway with six or seven tomatoes for sale, which her husband grew. She died in her seventies. I don't know why.

Old Mrs. Coster: Reminded me of Mrs. Tiggy-Winkle. After school, Anne and I would step off the bus and begin our walk down the turnpike toward home. "Let's see Mrs. Coster," who lived six houses up from ours. Anne and I would run across Mrs. Coster's lawn, knock on her door. There she would be in the frame of the screen. "Why, children, I hoped you'd come. I've made gingersnaps." And we'd walk along the little dark hall into Mrs. Coster's kitchen and find two plates on the table waiting for us: one for Anne and one for me, three cookies on each plate.

I pass a cemetery each day on my drive to work. Tombstones, crosses, concrete angels, mark each grave. Who were those people? Did they, too, like chocolate? Sing in their loneliness? Sell tomatoes? Have big noses? Dance? Love? Laugh?

I dislike the long obituaries of the rich and famous. They never tell me what I really want to know.

Squeezed
Into a
Small Place

The only sound in the house at the moment is made by the furnace as it burns the oil that is being pumped into the flames. Roe is attending a women's council meeting, and the three children are asleep.

And I don't like cremation.

The body of an ancient man was recently discovered in an ice floe in the Arctic. Anthropologists are excited about the tools and clothes found on his body. The photograph of the corpse is a ghastly thing: skin shriveled, teeth protruding, arms and legs bent in awkward positions.

For many years, for each family birthday, my mother would place the cake on a musical cake platter. As my mother pressed a small lever under the plate, the cake would begin to spin slowly to the tune of "Happy Birthday."

Moses, my cat, died when I was ten, and I buried him in the backwoods, just beyond the split oak tree. After I placed the final layer of earth upon the stiff body, I covered the freshly opened ground with a flat rock. Then I sat upon the rock for an hour or so.

In July, Michael discovered the Big Dipper. Since that evening he has included in his evening routine (after brushing his teeth, after being read to, after kisses) a walk to his bedroom window. Last night he introduced me to his observations.

"Daddy! The Big Dipper! I know where it is!"

As Michael and I looked through the window, all we saw was our own reflections, staring back at us.

"You gotta turn the lights out!" Michael affirmed.

I turned out the lights. We still couldn't see the night sky.

Just as I was about to make the suggestion, Michael began pressing his two hands against the window frame. I gave it a quick jab, and the window slid up.

"If you push the screen up too, you can see it even better," Michael knew.

As the screen slowly scratched upward, the darkness began to take on shape: the neighbor's house, the trees, the telephone wires, and then: "See—there, Daddy, right where I left it."

Between two trees, the Big Dipper tilted its tail down toward the south, right where Michael had left it.

From a distance, the surface of our planet looks blue and white and smooth to the touch. I am glad it is round, a blue circle without a beginning and without an end.

When I die, I would like to be buried in the earth. All that I am attracted to, all that I choose to love, seems to suggest things that are gentle: the roundness of the globe, the feel of my small son's hand in mine as we try to pry open a window, the weight of my cat as I carried him through the woods, over the skunk cabbage and ferns; poetry, the color of birthday candles, the last movements of a man held in a block of ice, the gray tail of the dead squirrel I saw on my trip home from work. The remains of our bodies mingling with the earth seems more gentle to me than the idea of flames and heat consuming what is left of our impermanent selves.

I just turned the furnace off. It is only the first weeks of autumn. The children are warm under their blankets. When Roe returns from her meeting, we will quickly ascend the stairs. I'll flick the furnace on again in the morning. Tonight I'd just like to be wrapped in life and quilts, squeezed into a small place beside my family under the seven stars of the Big Dipper, and that's how I'd like to be buried someday.

Faith

I received a telephone call from an insurance agent. He wanted to visit my home and evaluate my policies and determine if I needed more protection.

The man arrived on the agreed-upon evening with his calculator, his reference books, and his guides. After he read through my policies, he found that the house was underinsured, the car was underinsured, my life was underinsured, my children and my wife were underinsured. "Oh, you are in the legal limits on all your policies, but what would happen if you suddenly died?"

"Well, Roe is a bright, hardworking woman. She would have to give up her hard work and great responsibilities at home and create an income."

"But," the insurance agent said, his voice serious, "your wife would be denied the economic levels of comfort she was used to."

"My wife is perfectly capable of deciding what economic level of comfort is appropriate for her family under any circumstances."

"But your car—if you smash the car, without collision how could you afford to replace it, with your salary? I'd recommend you up your car insurance."

"My car is an object, like any other thing. It can be replaced for fifteen times less than you suggest I pay you over the years. Besides, God protects us."

"Mr. de Vinck, what if your house burns down tomorrow?"

"Our house is fully insured against such a disaster. The bank requires such insurance."

"But they only require such insurance to cover the outstanding dollar amount of what you owe them. They aren't too interested in rebuilding your house."

"Well," I answered, "houses do burn down, and it is a terrible thing, but I think the chances are in my favor that the house won't burn down. It's been sitting on this foundation for over forty years, and I haven't smelled smoke yet."

"And, Mr. de Vinck, what if you die?"

"You already asked me that question. According to your actuarial studies, I am a good risk. You can take my money for many, many years, and the chances are that I'll live a long time. I'll take a chance and believe your own figures. The statistics say that you won't be paying my wife and children any great sums of money, because I'll outlive any policy you can write."

"What about your retirement? Surely you would like to invest a portion of your salary in a pension plan?"

"So you want to sell me a life insurance policy because I am going to die young and leave my wife and starving children behind with a house that will soon burn to the ground, *and* you want me to buy into a retirement plan because I'll need the extra cash when I'm sixty-five?"

"But, Mr. de Vinck, you surely believe in some form of insurance, don't you?"

"If I died today, my wife would very capably continue to feed our children, love our children, sustain our children."

"But what if you both died?"

"I'd like to see the statistics on *that* coincidence, and even if it happened, I have two brothers and two sisters, who would immediately take my children into their homes. That's insurance."

"But what if your brothers and sisters fight over your estate and the adoption issues and—"

"You just don't get it, do you?"

"You need insurance, lots of insurance, Mr. de Vinck."

"Many years ago, I was a lonely young man. I was a graduate student in New York City. I longed to be in love. I longed for someone to be in love with me. That summer, I joined my parents on their annual vacation in central Canada. In this particular town, there is a small chapel at the top of a hill. It is really a shrine to a local priest who died in the service of his people. It is a one-room building, with just enough space for six pews on each side and an altar and a blue vase full of fresh flowers.

"That summer, I walked up the hill alone, opened the door of the chapel, said a prayer. Just before I stepped out into the sun, I stopped at the chapel door and pulled my wallet from my back pocket. Then I pulled out my college ID card with my photograph stamped below my student number. I lifted the card and placed it on the beam above the door, then I asked God if he could within the year introduce me to my wife. I planned to return one year later with my wife and retrieve my college card.

"Well, a year passed, and I hadn't met my wife. I once again took the long walk up the hill to the little chapel. Yes, the card was still there above the door, under a layer of dust and dead spiders. So I prayed again that God would introduce me to my wife within the year, and promised that she and I would return together to retrieve the card and give thanks.

"During the fall of that second year, I met Roe. We were engaged in six months. The following summer, we joined my parents on their annual vacation in central Canada. Roe and I walked up the long, steep hill to the chapel with twelve pews. The card was no longer there."

"But, Mr. de Vinck, what does this have to do with insurance?"

"You just don't understand, do you? The blue vase, it was still there, and Roe and I filled it with wildflowers: black-eyed susans, mullein, chicory."

The insurance salesman didn't use his calculator once that evening.

Life's Secrets

in the

Neighborhood

remember my first philosophical conversation. Barry, a fellow lifeguard, was driving me home one Sunday evening. We were seventeen years old.

"I can't wait for the summer to end," Barry said quietly as he turned into my driveway. It had been a long day.

"Oh, I don't know. College, leaving home—all that makes me a bit sad," I answered.

"Not me." Barry was driving barefoot. "I can't wait to get out of this place. I've been here since eighth grade. I'd like to travel."

Barry was reading the poems of Walt Whitman's *Leaves of Grass*.

"I'm not sure traveling is so terrific. What's so bad about this place?" I wasn't sure Barry was listening to me, but then he spoke about things I had never given thought to before.

"You gotta learn about the world. You gotta see lots of things to get a feeling for everything. You know the Whitman poem 'Song of the Open Road,' where it goes: 'I take to the open road, healthy, free, the world before me.' "

"Well, I don't know about Whitman," I said, "but I think all there is to know about the world can be discovered right here in town."

Barry laughed out loud. "In this town? Are you kidding? What about different cultures, Chris, and languages and places?"

I was annoyed that Barry laughed, so I qualified my position. "I even bet you can discover all there is to know about the world right here on this block."

"That's stupid, Chris. See you tomorrow at the lake."

After I pushed the car door shut, Barry drove off into the darkness and I stepped into the house—healthy, free, the world before me.

Twenty-six years later, I still believe that there aren't any hidden truths waiting for me in China, or Africa, or Australia. For the past three days, I have been watching the mushrooms appearing in the grass.

The weather this July has been humid, full of sudden rain. I wish I knew the name of the mushrooms. They are cream in color and sit between the green blades of grass. I like to lean over and look under the heads of the mushrooms and touch the thin ribs.

Recently a woman from our street stepped out of her house. "Chris." She called me over. "I have to tell you what Michael said to me. I was taking my usual walk, when he called out from your garden, 'I split a worm in half.' I asked him what he did with the worm, and he said, 'I dropped him in the sewer.' He then told me that the worm turned into a kangaroo, and he laughed and laughed."

I was sad to hear this story. I planned to tell Michael later that day that worms are small creatures and good for the soil.

Our neighbor to the right just gave birth to a girl, Caroline, seven pounds even, and I noticed that the moon is the size of the Cheshire Cat's smile tonight. Last night, David taught me how to find the North Star.

I like the sound of cooking pots clanging together as Roe and I wash the dishes together. There is a photograph of my grandmother on the wall above my desk here where I write. She died of cancer in her forties.

A neighbor's twenty-seven-year-old mentally disabled son waves to each of the children as they zoom past on their bicycles. I hear someone closing a window down the street and a dog barking. I kiss the children good night.

You can say what you like about culture and travel, you can say what you like about Europe or Africa, or the Orient or Oz. I think the children in Paris and the wives in Japan, the grandmothers dying of cancer in Melbourne, all know the soft touch of a mushroom and all see the crescent moon smiling in the same uncertain night.

W a r
C r y

I was returning to the dorm after a late-evening study session in the university library. The hall lights were dim. I stomped the snow off my shoes just before inserting my key in the lock of my room.

"Yeeeeah!" A long, loud, angry scream exploded to my left. I looked up from the key in my hand and saw someone rushing toward me, a bayonet twirling above his head.

"Yeeeeah!" The bayonet was against my throat. Fortunately, doors in the hall began to swing open. As the attacker pushed away from me and pressed himself against the wall, my neighbor stepped out of his room in his underwear and said, simply, "Oh, it's only you, Jerry." Without any concern about my life, my neighbor stepped into his room and shut the door.

Everyone else in the hall returned to his room and left me with Jerry and his bayonet. First, the intruder said, "I'm Jerry. I graduated three years ago." And then he passed out on the floor. After I dragged Jerry into my room and rolled him into bed, I stepped out and knocked on my neighbor's door. "Who is that guy?"

"Jerry? Everyone knows Jerry. He comes back to the dorm about twice a year. Did you see his face? Did you hear how he slurs his speech? Something about enemy fire in Vietnam. Most people around here think he's crazy. I think he's a pain in the butt." Then my neighbor's door closed for the second time that evening.

Many years ago, while driving to my first day of teaching in a rural section of northern New Jersey, I nearly drove off the road. I made a slow turn around a bend, when, suddenly, a pterodactyl flew about twenty feet above me, from left to right. I was startled: The creature's body, the way it held its head, and its wingspan looked exactly like the illustrations I had seen in the dinosaur books of my childhood.

I must add that I had never seen a blue heron until I made that turn in the road. For a few seconds, I actually thought I saw the famous flying dinosaur that hangs from the ceiling of many museums of natural history.

When I realized that I was looking at a blue heron, I was nearly as impressed as if it were the pterodactyl. To watch such a large bird fly in slow motion, a bird I had never seen before, was like watching something that had escaped from the garden of Paradise.

Jerry had sprung up at me as quickly as the blue heron. The morning after his "attack" in the hallway, I invited him to breakfast. We drove to a local diner.

"Most people keep away from me. I was happy here in college. That's why I like coming back. Something left behind, perhaps, something I'd like to find again. Sorry about last night."

Jerry told me a little about the Vietnam War, about his girlfriend, who abandoned him on his return. He showed me pictures from his wallet. He thanked me for breakfast, shook my hand, and left. I never saw Jerry again, and I do not know what happened to him.

Someday, brush your open hand against the names engraved on the Vietnam Memorial in Washington. You will not discover politics or war or history under your fingertips, but rather you will find sons and daughters, fathers and brothers, who died through circumstances or duty or fear or love of country or courage. I never fought in a war because of circumstances or duty or fear or love of country or courage.

Jerry frightened me that night as I returned from the library in my comfortable and safe college campus, because it was the very first time war meant anything to me.

Daffodils

and

the Devil

If suffering is such a powerful force in the world, why doesn't it affect the condition of the daffodils that have bloomed outside my window this week?

On the front page of the *New York Times* today, there is a photograph of a man embracing a few loaves of bread close to his chest. He is looking beyond the camera. He is a refugee of war, hungry, on the run. He doesn't know that his picture sits on my coffee table this evening. The bread will sustain him until tomorrow.

This evening, I called my mother on the telephone simply to say hello. She said to me, "Chris, remember I told you about Father Ignatius from India?"

Father Ignatius discovered, a number of years ago, one of my mother's books of poetry, loved her work, wrote her a letter telling her so, all the way from India. Over the years, my mother and Father Ignatius wrote back and forth about faith and family, books and literature. He even developed a special love for Karen. "Father Ignatius loved so much the picture of Karen which I sent him," my mother said. "He prays for her each night."

Somewhere in the distant country of India, a holy man was praying for my daughter. I liked that.

"Chris, I received a letter today from India, telling me that Father Ignatius was murdered, stabbed repeatedly in a robbery."

Daffodils. The yellow flower sits upon a thin green stem and sways back and forth at the smallest breeze. I sat out with the daffodils tonight on the front stoop. There is a cold front pushing its way down from the north. The unusual heat we have been experiencing in this early spring is abating.

I never met Father Ignatius from India, but he prayed for my daughter. The long arms of the devil stretched across the ocean, halfway around the globe, all the way from India, and tried to kiss the cheeks of my daughter after thrusting a knife again and again into the body of a good man. But do you see? Father Ignatius prayed for Karen, and he continues to send along his salutations if you believe in heaven and justice and the power of God, which can easily be forgotten in this world that claims to be modern but sits on the fragile edge, balanced between all that is good and all that is evil.

I believe we hunger for the good. I believe in the sustenance of beauty and in the destructive power of the devil's reach.

Somewhere in India, there is an abandoned photograph of my daughter. She sleeps tonight under her pink sheets, while the daffodils sway back and forth in the darkness.

Love

It is obvious: we need to be loved. There is a wonderful scene in the movie *Hook* in which Peter Pan returns to Never-Never-Land. He is with the lost boys. The boys don't recognize Peter because he grew up, sounds old, looks different.

Then one of the littlest boys places a hand on each side of Peter's face. The child looks directly into Peter's eyes and says, "Oh, there you are, Peter."

The boy found his Peter Pan. If you look deep inside yourself, you will discover or rediscover the person that is lovable. If you look deep inside the person next to you, you will be able to discover or rediscover what can be loved about that person.

This is one of the things I knew for sure when I started my teaching career. I could see something wonderful in all my students. I remember Joy, who was the saddest girl I ever met. She didn't talk. She never looked up from her desk, never looked you right in the eye. But this hurt young person was perhaps one of the most beautiful students I met. In her silence, in her pain (I later learned that she was an abused child), in the morning of the fifth week of school, my students were taking turns reading *The Glass Menagerie*. It was, again, Joy's turn. I was expecting that she would, as always, refuse to read and that I, as always, would simply move on to the next student in her row. But for some reason, Joy began reading:

" 'Little articles of it, they're ornaments mostly! Most of them are little animals made out of glass, the tiniest little animals in the world. Mother calls them a glass menagerie!' "

Joy continued to read Laura's part for fifteen minutes, with clarity, power, confidence. After she finished, she pulled her face up from the book, looked at me, and smiled.

You see? Joy. Someone to love.

I discovered one of the most striking examples of this need for love in Tolstoy's story "The Death of Ivan Ilyich."

Here was a man who was unreflective. He simply moved through his life as he believed he ought to, according to what society said. When he was young he pursued women and wine. When it was time to settle down, he selected a woman to marry and aimed his energies toward advancement in his career. His major interests in life were to attain the next promotion and play cards with his friends. Things were going just as they were supposed to, until Ivan Ilyich learned he had a fatal illness.

His was a long, slow death. He had been slowly dying all along, even before the illness, but he didn't know this. He pushed his wife away from him. He took no interest in his son and daughter. He was a man who cared for himself and his own comfort and success, but then something happened.

During his dying he endured great emotional pain. He couldn't understand why he had to suffer and die. He was desperately seeking answers to his own life, ending so prematurely. A darkness was enfolding him. He could not understand the world, his life, and most of all his own death. All was nearly lost, then something happened.

As he was very close to death, a young boy entered the room. The man was in turmoil, throwing himself deeper and deeper into an agony he could not understand. The young boy was the dying man's son. The child reached over and took his father's hand. The boy then pressed his father's hand into his own face, and the boy wept. Seeing this, the father suddenly understood. At that moment he understood. He saw a light, a bright light. He watched his son weep, and the father knew that there, weeping before him, was the world and all the world had to offer us human beings: love. The boy simply loved his father. That is all. That is everything, and everything to come.

Small Deaths
Along the Way

I was walking in mid-Manhattan, on my way home from a meeting, when I found myself surrounded by five children. They were nine or ten years old.

The air was humid. One of the children spoke to me directly. "Mister, what's your name?"

I didn't know what to say.

"Mister, what's your name?" he asked again. That is when I began to notice the other children. I felt little hands groping through my jacket, through my back pockets. I reached behind me and found a small palm and fingers already coiled around my wallet.

"Mister, you got a name?"

I brushed the hands away. "What are you doing?" I asked anxiously.

One of the children spit in my face, just before he and the others ran down the street and disappeared.

As I wiped my brow, I was reminded once again of how troubled their lives are when children come to believe that the world is a brutal place.

The first time I saw this lesson taught was in my freshman year in college. I read in the school newspaper that the local orphanage would accept student volunteers to help out on weekends. I decided to join four friends and see what we might be able to do.

The home, five miles from the university, was set back from the main highway. Surrounded by a rough lawn and oak trees, it was ringed by a driveway of crushed stone.

We drove up to the main building and stepped out of the car, to be greeted by a large woman in a long beige dress. Her hair was tucked under a yellow kerchief.

"The children are out back. They've just had lunch. It's their free time. Why don't you walk over and introduce yourselves?"

My friends and I walked along the crushed-stone path, passed a barn, turned the corner of the main house. The five of us stopped. At least thirty children, ranging in age from two to thirteen, were running, shouting, jumping rope, and laughing, until one by one, they saw us standing in the shadows.

All was silent.

A few children, some of the oldest, stepped toward us, then the younger children followed. A girl—she must have been eleven or twelve—reached out her hand toward me and asked, "What's your name?"

"Chris," I answered as we shook hands.

"I'm Brenda. My parents are dead."

Suddenly the ropes began to swing round and round again, the shouting and laughing returned to the courtyard. For the first half hour we college students were asked to play catch, leapfrog, mother-may-I.

The more comfortable the children felt around us, the more affectionate they were. They jumped on us, insisted we give them piggyback rides. They tickled us. After Brenda and I were the last ones left in the wide circle of closed hands at the conclusion of a game similar to musical chairs, she gave me one of the sincerest embraces I've ever felt.

Brenda wore blue jeans, a gray sweater. Her hair was black, curled at the ends, and tangled with oak leaves. We all laughed and laughed, until a harsh buzz emanated from the loudspeaker attached to one of the trees.

The children stood up immediately and started walking back to the main house in silence. The woman who had greeted us at the main entrance held the door open for the children, then, with little grace, she stepped up to the five of us as we brushed the dirt and leaves from our hair and clothes.

"We don't allow the children to touch the guests. They will get too attached. You don't have to come here again."

She turned. I remember seeing loose hair brushing against the back of her neck from under her yellow kerchief as she walked up to the house. We were not invited back to the orphanage. I never saw Brenda again.

What has been placed between the giving heart and those in need? I felt the little hands frisking my clothes, and I was afraid. A child's hugging me in the excitement of an afternoon game turned out to be against the rules.

We need to allow our social institutions to teach children how to love and accept love; otherwise we create a world where people spit in your face and press their fingers against the harsh buzzer.

And the
Dolphins
Leap

In the late summer of 1991, Roe and I spent two days at Beach Haven, New Jersey, with three other couples. We had planned this weekend with our friends nearly four months before.

Our three children stayed with neighbors; the cat was provided for. I was tired, disappointed about the weak response to my new book, overwhelmed with the beginning of a new teaching year. For the first time in my fifteen years of teaching, I did not want to be in the classroom.

To spend two days at the seashore seemed to be a good idea. When we arrived, the first thing I did was to watch the ocean waves crash repetitiously against the sand, then Joe, Greg, Tom, and I, like four little boys, ran upon the beach and dove into the curling water. Our wives set up the chairs and umbrellas.

I had never swum in the ocean before. I was startled by the taste of salt, though it was to be expected. What I didn't expect was the size of the waves.

"You have to dive under them at just the right angle and time," Tom warned as we bobbed up and down with the tide.

Whoosh! It was as though a suitcase lid had crashed down upon me, a wet, heavy suitcase lid, for I was quickly in darkness, being tossed around. After a strange rippling motion passed over my body, I was finally able to stand up.

"I liked that," I called out.

For the next hour, we four men dove into the waves, jumped over the white foam, talked about our lives, our sons and daughters, our wives, and floated on our backs like content sea otters wrapped in warm kelp. I didn't know that two hours inland, Carly was dying.

I remember the first time I met Carly. Two years earlier, a student had popped into my classroom just to introduce herself. Ever since, Carly made it part of her routine to stop in every now and then to say hi. If she missed me, she would write a small note saying hello, signing it with her name and a smiley face. I taped these notes on the wall.

During those two years I realized that Carly made it a point to visit many, many teachers, the principal, her friends in and out of school. To say that she was a child of light would trivialize the true character of this extraordinary young woman. I say she was extraordinary because of her intellect (she was accepted at Holy Cross College in their premed program). I say she was extraordinary because of her beauty, her athletic ability, her sense of goodness and fun and seriousness and friendship. But the way she dealt with the cancer that was discovered in her sixteen-year-old legs and lungs equals the triumph of any historic or modern hero.

When Carly first told me of her illness she wept in my little office, pulled out a pencil and paper, drew a huge smiley face, wrote in bold letters, "Hi, Mr. de Vinck," plunked it on my desk, and left.

As Carly began to lose her blond hair because of the medical treatments, she would come to school with a pink bow tied neatly around the very last strands. Can you imagine the courage it took Carly to stand before her bedroom mirror alone in the morning and watch the daily changes in her body? Can you imagine the courage it took to reach across her dresser, take the comb in her hand, slowly collect the thin bits of hair that were left, and tie that ribbon into a delicate bow?

"I didn't want to come to school with a wig on," she said one afternoon. "I just want to be me, Carly, like always."

As the year progressed, Carly was more and more unable to attend school. She had surgery on her leg. She began to use crutches, but on the days she was in school, she always, always smiled, teased you, came up with the right answers in class. Carly was Carly, like always.

I hadn't seen her for a number of weeks. I was in my literature class. We were reading *Othello* when, at one point, the door swung open and Carly walked in. She said hello to everyone with her usual smile, then she stood beside me and placed a picture on my desk.

It was a glossy photograph. To the left was one of my former students in his West Point dress uniform. To the right was another cadet in his crisp uniform. Standing between these two handsome young men stood Carly. She wore a long camel-color winter coat. She had a yellow blouse buttoned at her neck. Her long hair framed her face with exquisite simplicity and grace.

"Wasn't my hair beautiful, Mr. de Vinck?" Carly said as I looked up from the photograph.

On Sunday morning in Beach Haven, two friends in our group decided to wake up early and watch the sun rise. Everyone else was invited, but we others chose to sleep in.

At the breakfast table, Linda and Greg said, "Chris, we almost came to wake you up. As we were waiting for the sun, twenty or thirty dolphins leaped up into the air, just about in the same spot where you guys were swimming yesterday!"

On Sunday, September 8, 1991, my young friend Carly died at home in her room, in the presence of her family, who loved her, and the dolphins leaped above the waves at Beach Haven, New Jersey.

Songs
of
Christmas

CANTO VII

They said hard wood was good for burning
(Little smoke, the flame clean),
Out back where the talk brought in the
Wolves and bears across Lapland.

I heard strange tales about
The snow becoming like the sea.

I was placed among men with gold in their teeth;
One stood and claimed the territory,
Brought down the whole tract
With a single blast from his gun:
"I've got the hide and claws to prove it."

And round the Christmas bowl they stood:
Uncles, neighbors, a hero or two.

I was a boy, remembered the bells
On the sledge, the closing of doors,
Leaned back against the wall,
Knew the brave talk and names of the
Constellations and the light of Arcturus,

But I kept my hands in my pockets,
Laughed in the right places,
Tossed an oak log into the fire
And watched the sparks quietly rise—
A thousand stars shooting up the flue
In one quick motion

To die in the blue December night.

The
Christmas
Goose

When I was eight, the day before Christmas was no different than in most other homes. Christmas cards grew like vines along the doorframe of the living room; the wreath on the front door bounced against the glass with a scratching sound each time the door was opened and closed; packages of chocolate or fruit or shoes arrived in the mail.

The shoes were from my grandmother. Each summer, before she returned to Belgium after her summer visit, she would ask me to stand on a sheet of typing paper while my father traced the outline of my foot with a sharp pencil, so my grandmother would have the exact measurements for my Christmas shoes.

I never wore those shoes, because Belgian fashions and my grandmother's ideas of appropriate footwear never matched the popularity of Keds and P-F Flyers.

On the day before Christmas, the last thing anyone wanted to do was get in the way of my mother. My brothers and sisters and I were forbidden to eat any of the freshly baked cookies. We were not allowed in my mother's bedroom, because that was where the presents, some already wrapped and some not, were kept.

Above all else, no one wanted to disturb my mother in the kitchen. Great and dark events in my childhood began in the kitchen and spilled out into the rest of the house, followed by my mother screaming and waving a wooden spoon.

Often, on those difficult days, I felt it was best to run outside, where it was hard to get myself in trouble by building a snowman or snapping icicles from the garage gutter and eating them like candy sticks.

On this particular Christmas Eve, it had snowed and snowed in the early morning. The new accumulation looked like freshly baked loaves of bread on top of the bird feeder and the garbage cans. The white lawn reflected the sun's glare into my eyes. It was just the right type of day for tracking rabbits.

After each snowfall, I believed I could follow the tracks of a rabbit and find out where it lived, or at least where it spent the better part of the day.

I pulled on my blue coat with the matted fur, wrapped my scarf around my neck, forced a wool cap over my head, and buckled my brother's black boots on my feet. I was ready.

My mother and Christmas faded behind me in a wash of color as I stepped into the bleached yard. I spotted a fresh set of tracks, which quickly led me down the lawn, under the bare apple tree, and into the woods, closed and gray-looking.

The tracks of this rabbit were like all the rest: the rear paws were long; the front ones small and narrow. I followed the tracks through the woods, over a frozen pond, under a wire fence. Just as I was beginning to believe the tracks would soon lead me to my destination, just as I was sure that at any moment I would find this particular rabbit huddled under a bush, waiting for me with a smile and a cup of tea, the tracks became hopelessly crisscrossed with another set, then another and another. Five, six, perhaps seven tracks ran upon each other and off in different directions. I lost my rabbit. The hunt was over.

I didn't feel it was safe yet to return to the house, and besides,

I wasn't really cold, so I scooped up a little snow and licked it. Then I decided to walk to the swamp.

The swamp was an old, abandoned celery farm with irrigation ditches and wide fields, which often flooded. My sisters, brothers, and I would ice-skate there in the winter and hunt for turtles and fish in the summer. To reach the swamp, I had to cross a small footbridge, skirt the edge of a frozen lettuce field, and then step along a narrow path until I could set my feet onto the ice.

I liked the swamp. I liked to snap the dry stalks of the milkweed. I liked to run on the ice without skates and slide through the fresh snow. I liked the open space where there were no mothers and where I was about the tallest thing around.

As I climbed up the bank of the path and shook the snow off the top of my boots, I noticed in the distance a large sheet of white paper flapping up and down. Or was it paper? It was something worth investigating. Investigating is the duty of eight-year-old boys.

I slid down the bank and onto the ice. It was smooth and clear. I could see goldfish swimming under the glassy film, flicking their tails slowly, pushing their fins back and forth.

As I began to walk, I lost sight of the white object I had seen flapping in the wind.

A red-winged blackbird balanced itself on the tip of a reed. A cluster of milkweed pods rattled as they brushed against my passing legs. After walking a few moments, I finally stepped up to a small mound of earth, and there, directly below me, caught in the brambles, pressed against the frozen earth, was the biggest, whitest goose I had ever seen, beating one wing up and down in distress. As I approached, the goose stopped thrashing its wing. Its head was laying on the dark earth, its beak was open, its eyes were moist and running.

I looked around. No one was there.

The first thing I wanted to do was touch that goose. I bent over and stretched out my hand. The goose flapped its wing and nearly knocked me over. It raised its head for a moment, then collapsed, exhausted.

Again I bent down, but this time I whispered, "Nice goose. I won't hurt you. Nice goose." I stroked its neck and back. I was surprised. The goose felt hard and bony, not soft and plush as I had imagined. It stopped beating its wing. It closed its eyes. I thought it had died.

Then the goose struggled up again and stood for a moment. Its other wing looked twisted, broken, useless, hanging like a crooked window shutter. The goose collapsed to the ground and closed its eyes again.

I looked for other geese. I looked for a trap, or a hunter, or a boy with a stone, wondering how the goose had been injured. Then I leaned down and lifted the goose with both my arms. I was going to bring it home.

I was surprised and dismayed to discover how heavy it was. A goose in flight is a lovely thing; crumpled on the ground, it is an awkward, heavy collection of neck and wings and legs. I didn't know how to carry it.

I lifted its body in one arm like a sack of potatoes and supported the drooping neck on my other arm, the head resting in my hand.

All I knew about geese came from pictures in my old nursery school books—the *V* in the fall sky—and from sounds in the children's zoo. But I felt I knew everything there was to know about the care of an injured animal: feed it, give it plenty of water, and keep it warm. That is what I was going to do.

I was a little boy of eight in the middle of a large, empty swamp where the water was frozen and snow covered the reeds and ice. I pretended that I was a trapper, a fur trader carrying something heavy, a prize catch, a goose to be taken home and bragged about. I believed I would be looked upon as as hero.

What I could not imagine was what my mother would say about my goose. I decided not to tell her.

I carried my goose across the ice, over the goldfish, up the road, back along the frozen lettuce field. I stepped across the scattered rabbit tracks, back through the woods, up the lawn. The goose did not move, did not strike out, and did not make a noise, but it was breathing. I could feel its lungs expand and contract in my grasp.

Behind the garage of our house, we had an old chicken coop, which we children used as our clubhouse, bakery, gas station, bank, castle. It was all our own, and no one but us went in there. That is where I decided to keep the goose.

When I entered the coop, I was glad to see that the old rug we had laid down in the summer was still there. It would be warmer than the floor. I placed my goose on the rug, expecting its immediate recovery and gratitude. Instead it dropped its neck, its head, its wings, its legs, in one helpless motion. I couldn't yet feed it or give it anything to drink, but I could make it warm, and I had a plan.

The day before, my mother and father had brought out the Christmas boxes from the attic, those magic containers with bulbs and lights and a star, which we never saw except at Christmas. The boxes also contained the only extension cords in the house. They were used each year for the tree and the porch lights. I needed the extension cords to bring power for the electric heater to the goose.

I returned to the house, afraid I had goose feathers sticking out of my hair. I tried not to be noticed, not to get in anybody's way.

"Brush the snow from your clothes before taking them off."

"Yes, Mom." I ran out of the kitchen and up to the top of the stairs, where the Christmas boxes were stacked. The tall box contained the colored lights. The cookie tins with pictures of poinsettias and holly leaves contained the ornaments. The flat boxes were filled with extension cords. I took three flat boxes, leaving the last one, hoping that no one would miss those I had taken.

I carried the three boxes to the basement and sat on the washing machine, where, for the first time since I had found the goose, I stopped. Closing my eyes, I prayed, "Please, God, don't let my goose die."

My father's workbench stood against the back wall, and there I found the heater under a pile of scrap wood. I brought the heater, the extension cords, and my courage to the basement window, connected the cords, and plugged one end into the nearest outlet. After shoving out the heater, I was able to close the window on the wire, so the basement looked as it was supposed to look.

I ran out the back door, picked up the heater, and started unwinding the tangled cord from the basement window, across the lawn, up to the chicken coop. As I went, I covered the wire with snow, so no one could see my trail.

When I stepped into the coop, I found that my goose still hadn't moved, still hadn't recovered. It just breathed and breathed. Its eyes remained glazed, its beak open. I lugged in the heater and turned the setting to High. Within a few moments, the coils glowed and the fan blew a stream of warm air toward the goose.

I covered the windows with old newspapers and sat next to my goose. For the rest of the afternoon, I stroked its long neck and stiff feathers.

Just before dark, I managed to bring the goose a slice of bread from the kitchen and a dish of water. Then I left the light glowing from the hot coils, the sound whirring from the blowing fan . . . and my goose, dying in the middle of the floor.

In the kitchen, there was much carrying on. The tree was up. The ornaments were being prepared. But my mother had discovered that some of the extension cords were missing.

"This one box might—and I say might—have enough wire to

reach the tree, but the porch lights can't go on without the others."

No one knew where they were, and no one asked me; clearly I was too little to have anything to do with them.

"I'll go to the store and buy some more," my father suggested meekly.

"It's Christmas Eve. The stores are closed," snapped my mother.

My father then suggested borrowing from the neighbors, but my mother decided that, after all, the porch lights were not important, and the extension cords were "probably in the attic and we'll find them tomorrow." So we all began to decorate the tree, play records, and drink apple juice. I forgot all about my goose until I went to bed.

"Now I lay me down to sleep. I pray the Lord my soul to keep. Guard me, Jesus, through the night, and wake me with the morning light. Amen. And please help our goose in the chicken coop. Amen again. Good night. Merry Christmas." Then I slept.

Christmas morning. My stocking was at the foot of the bed, filled with a candy cane, tin soldiers, magnetic bugs, and a wood top. The room was bright. I looked out the window and was surprised to see that during the night there had been another heavy snowfall. The trees were drooping with fresh snow. I realized that my room was cold. I jumped out of bed, dressed, and ran downstairs. Almost everybody was in the living room.

"Mom, it's freezing in my room."

"Your father is taking care of it. We have plenty of wood for the fireplace. The snow knocked down a few power lines. We don't have electricity."

"Oh," I answered, remembering that this had happened before and that it was fun to use candles and the fireplace, and, yes, the room was warm enough, and besides, today was Christmas, and . . . Then I remembered my goose, the extension cords, the heater, and . . . no electricity!

"My goose!" I shouted. "My goose!" I jumped from my seat, ran through the kitchen toward the back door.

"What did you say?" my mother demanded. "Where are you going? You need your coat! Come back here!"

But I didn't listen. I ran to the door and out into the yard. The heavy snow made running difficult. I felt as if I were struggling through a vat of taffy. I pumped my legs up and down, up and down, working my way as fast as I could to the chicken coop.

The door was blocked by a snowdrift. With my bare, cold hands I scratched and pulled the snow away. I tried to look through the cracks in the door, but I could see nothing inside. Newspaper covered the windows, and the snow's glare blinded me.

Finally the door was free. I stepped in and brushed the light out of my eyes. I looked all around. The bread was gone. The water was gone. . . . And there, sitting in the corner, in a very gooselike fashion, was my white goose, probably expecting an applause. I stepped close to it. It let me touch its warm head, its strong back, its strong wings—both of them!

I heard my brother in the background, screeching with devilish delight: "I found the extension cords! Boy, are you gonna get it!"

I heard my mother slamming the back door and my sister and my father calling my name. Then I stepped out of the chicken coop with the white goose cradled in my arms.

The True
Identity of
Santa Claus

It finally happened. Just as I tucked her covers under the mattress, Karen, who was about to press her cheek against her pillow, suddenly sat up, pulled her knees to her chest, and said, "Now, Daddy. I'm old enough. I have to know. Is Santa Claus real?"

Fathers are tested at the least-expected moments.

"What do you mean, Karen?"

"Well, I've been thinking. Is there a Santa Claus?"

Before I answered that question, I wanted to have a clear idea where Karen stood on the issue. "How would you feel if he didn't exist?"

"I wouldn't like that."

OK. Now I knew where this was heading. "Well, what do you think?"

"Well," Karen continued, with a voice that matched her serious intentions. "First of all, I've never seen flying reindeer."

"Karen, there are wandering tribes of people in Australia who have never seen an airplane. What do you think they would say if you told them that there is a machine that can help them fly over the clouds?"

"They probably wouldn't believe me. What's that got to do with reindeer?"

"Well, you haven't seen flying reindeer the same way those

people haven't seen an airplane, but the airplane does exist." I know I was stretching the point.

"OK. How can Santa Claus deliver all those presents at the same time?" Karen looked at me as if I were about to fail an exam.

"Well, there are certain things about Santa Claus that I don't understand either." Karen seemed to accept that.

(Someone told me a few days after this conversation that I should have explained to my daughter that Santa stopped time in the middle of Christmas Eve so that he could bring everyone the gifts. Good answer, I thought.)

"Well, I have a good reason why there must be a Santa Claus," Karen continued, perhaps trying to help me out. "Some of my friends are getting video games, bikes, CD players. Their parents can't afford all those presents, so Santa must give those kids some of the gifts. But I have another question: If no one has ever really seen Santa Claus, how do we know what he looks like?"

Yeah, Dad. Answer that one.

"Well, many people caught a glimpse of him, you know, as he was zooming off in the sleigh, or as he turned the corner in the living room. Then all these people met at a conference and pooled their information. It turned out that many people saw a red coat. Some people were pretty sure the person had a beard. More than half the people at the conference were convinced that the beard was white and that the fellow wore black boots. They invited an artist to the meeting, gave him all the bits of information, and, well, by putting all the pieces together the artist was able to paint a picture of Santa Claus."

Karen gave me the look she used when I tried to explain fractions to her.

"Is Santa Claus American?"

"What do you mean?" I asked. I wanted to laugh.

"Well, Jill, one of my best friends in school . . . her mother is from Korea and her father is from here. Jill doesn't have those pretty eyes like her mother, slanted a bit? But Jill's sister does?"

I wasn't exactly sure where Karen was going with this.

"Santa Claus goes all over the world, right?" Karen asked.

"Right."

"And he lives at the North Pole?"

"Yeah."

"Wouldn't children in Africa and Japan and all over expect Santa Claus to look like their grandfather?"

After a few minutes, Karen and I both figured out that Santa Claus was a combination of all people. His skin was dark and light, his eyes slanted just a bit, his nose was just a little big, and he spoke every language.

"How does 'Ho! Ho! Ho!' sound in French?"

"I'm not sure, Karen."

"Well, I know there's no Easter Bunny. I heard David telling Mickey two years ago that the Easter Bunny is really Mrs. Patterson in a rabbit costume."

"Time for bed."

"OK. I love you. Good night." Karen kissed me, then gently placed her head on her pillow.

"I love you too, my angel," I said as I turned out the light.

I walked downstairs, explained to Roe why it had taken so long to put Karen to bed, then I walked to my basement office and began my writing for the evening.

After answering three letters, typing out a new poem, and making a few corrections on my latest manuscript, I switched off the lights in my office, climbed the stairs, unplugged the Christmas candles from each window in the living room. Then I walked up to the bedrooms.

I unplugged the candles in David's and Michael's room. I stepped into Karen's room, unplugged her candle, leaned over my sleeping daughter, kissed her cheek, and then I whispered, "I am Santa Claus."

Gifts

A toy brown bear tried to tell me a story as I walked past his display in the department store this afternoon. Cost: $69. For $119 I can buy my son a five-foot-long red motorized fire engine. An entire city of plastic blocks and people and signs can be had for $89 with the rebate.

Forget the North Pole and the image of little men hammering wheels to wooden cars and painting rouge upon the smooth cheeks of rag dolls. We have warehouse toy stores, stuffed animals the size of my car, video adventures, remote-controlled cars, planes, boats. We can buy dolls that grow, shrink, kiss, crawl, dance, wet, drink, swim, sleep, cry . . . each one $20, $30, $40.

The two Christmas gifts that meant the most to me when I was a child were both inexpensive and made of wood: a gift from my mother and a gift from my father. Now that I look back, I see that it wasn't even the things themselves that, to this day, hold me to their memories.

One November, I was shopping with my mother. We entered one shop, the Scandinavian Import Store. Sitting on a glass shelf, among different wood figures, was a troll. He was tall as a book, wore a red hat and a white apron. He held a flower in his right hand. This creature had no purpose except to delight a small boy. I asked my mother if she could buy it.

"It's $8.95, really much too expensive," she said.

Three brothers, two sisters, $8.95. Of course she was right, and I returned the wood figure to the shelf.

On Christmas morning, I opened a white box, unfolded the tissue paper, and there he was: red hat, apron, the little flower.

Each year, my wife takes the Scandinavian troll out of the Christmas boxes and places him on top of our living room clock.

I received the following Christmas the second gift that held the same quality of magic and permanence.

My brothers and sisters and I were unwrapping presents, looking at name tags: "This one's for Bruno. Annie, here's one for you."

"Christopher." My father handed me a gift about the width and length of a shoe box, which was tightly wrapped.

I was struggling with the tape and ribbon. My father leaned over to help me. I remember his hands: the veins bulging out from under his skin; the long fingers. He was close to me, nearly embracing me, like a great bear. This is what I remember.

When the paper and bow and tape were loose enough, I unraveled the whole affair, lifted the lid from the box. I found a wooden soldier on his back in a painted red uniform, waiting for me.

"It's a bank too, Christopher. See the little key?" His head was attached to his body with a thick gray spring. He wore a black helmet, a black belt. His buttons were dabs of gold paint. Today he sits on my desk, to the left of my books by Robert Frost, Dylan Thomas, and Louis MacNeice.

I do have my biases. If a Christmas gift for a child isn't under ten dollars and isn't made of wood, well, then, it can't be worth much.

I have, too, the memories of my mother stretching a budget, and my father stretching out his long arms toward me.

It is really the embrace that a child seeks on Christmas morning, and the delight.

Dancing
Angels

Roe taught second-grade religion class at our church on Monday nights. Karen was in Roe's class.

One Monday evening after supper, Karen was bouncing around the house like a pogo stick in anticipation of the religion class that was to begin in half an hour.

"I'm so excited, Daddy," she yelled. "Tonight we're going to practice for the Christmas pageant!"

Each year, the children perform the Nativity at the ten o'clock mass on Christmas Day.

"That's wonderful, Karen."

Soon enough Roe and Karen slipped on their winter coats, or should I say that Roe slipped on her coat and Karen dove into hers and began to run toward the front door.

" 'Bye, Daddy. See you later!"

"Goodbye, Karen."

As the car pulled out from the driveway, I walked from room to room and plugged in the electric candles we display at each window. Christmas is a season of lights.

Later that evening, after Roe and Karen returned from the hour-long practice, I unplugged all the living room and dining room candles and carried a tired little girl to bed.

When Karen had brushed her teeth, pulled on her pink pajamas, and crawled under the bedcovers, I sat beside her.

Without warning, Karen looked up at me, and her eyes began to water.

"Daddy," she said.

"What's wrong, Karen?"

"I don't want to be a dancing angel." Then she began to cry.

"Karen, why not?"

"We have to do these steps and hold hands in a circle, and I just don't want to be a dancing angel."

She could not control her weeping.

"Would you like to be a regular angel, then?" I was not getting the point.

"No." She sighed, shaking her head back and forth upon her pillow. Then she looked up at me, stopped her crying, and whispered "I wanted to be Mary."

Ah, Mary. That was it. Earlier in the evening, before she drove to church with Roe, Karen had anticipated the rehearsal, the excitement, the role assignments.

"Karen, my girl."

"I wanted to be Mary so much. You have to be in third or fourth grade to be Mary."

"The angels were important too," I said, trying to sound wise.

"Did they have to dance when Jesus was born?"

"Well, maybe when they were guiding the shepherds they danced a bit."

"I can't even twist my feet the way they want us to."

"You'll make a wonderful dancing angel."

"Will you be there, Daddy?"

"Of course I'll be there."

"OK. Let's say prayers."

And that is what we did, my daughter and I.

After we said the prayers, after I tucked Karen's blanket under the mattress, after I kissed her good night, she whispered, "Maybe I could be Mary next year."

"Perhaps, my girl. Next year. Good night, my angel."

"Good night, Daddy."

Before going to sleep later that evening, I decided to leave the Christmas candles glowing in Karen's bedroom for the rest of the night.

Dreaming
of Home

My grandmother died many years ago, but her dresses still hang in her closet at my parents' house. Her shoes are still neatly placed beside her closed umbrella.

Before my grandfather died, he bought a trellis and trained the roses to weave slowly up both sides and join together at the top in an embrace, completing the purpose of the trellis and fulfilling my grandfather's desire to leave something behind.

Things accumulate around us. The older we become, the less those things mean and the more we seem to look around for a true legacy of our existence.

When my mother's poodle died, I unclipped the tag from the dog's collar, climbed the tallest pine tree in the yard, and nailed the tag into the tree's trunk above the highest branch I could reach. I do not know why I did this.

One afternoon when I was a child, I was playing with a magnet. It must have been part of some board game. It was covered in plastic, was about the size of a man's thumb, and had the shape of a bee. I was playing with this bee magnet as I sat at the upright piano. I remember opening the piano to reveal the hammers and strings. I pinched the bee magnet between my thumb and index finger, slowly inserted my hand into the piano's inner works, and hung the plastic bee on one of the metal strings. I intended to strike the piano key that corresponded to the string that held the magnetic bee. I thought it would be fun to watch the bee slide downward against the vibration of the wire.

I hit the key. The hammer struck the proper note. Instead of wiggling slowly downward, the magnet jumped off the string and disappeared into the piano's intestines.

I knew that bee was stuck inside the piano. Thirty years later, I took apart the piano's works to retrieve the yellow bee.

On the desk where I write I have a glass jar. Inside that jar is my collection of dried rose petals from my parents' garden.

This December, I will celebrate my forty-fourth Christmas. All the Christmas days of my life were celebrated in the same house, before the same Christmas ornaments, the same fireplace, with the same Christmas music played over and over again, a day in Brigadoon, perhaps.

The Christmas rocks are under the front porch. Each Christmas, my father comes home with the Christmas tree. Each Christmas, my mother wraps a bucket in silver foil and places it in the same place in the living room. My father drags the tree into the house. He then steps out the front door, walks down the cement steps, turns right, then right again, stoops down, and rolls out five or six rocks the size of footballs. These are the rocks, the Christmas rocks, he uses to anchor the Christmas tree inside the bucket year after year.

We have a space probe hurling itself farther and farther from earth, deep into the distance, and we wildly dream of a message bouncing off the outer edges of time, a message of another life, other dimensions, other chemical combinations that will yield, perhaps, the secrets of immortality.

I believe eternity is a circle, not a straight line. I return to my mother and father's house this Christmas. I think about my father stooping down and reaching his hands into the darkness under the front porch and pulling out the common stones. I think of my mother placing the silver bucket upon the same ringed indentation that is pressed for all time upon the living room carpet.

Turning, turning. Yellow bees. Strange messages tacked in tall pine trees. An old woman's shoes, umbrellas. A trellis of white roses. We are meant to live in the present time, as we slowly roll over in our beds at night, dreaming of home.

Songs
of the
Circle

CANTO VIII

I look up through the trees
And see a god,
Or the eye of God,
Perhaps some artist's joke
In the night sky,
Made of paint and plaster,
A first attempt to
Re-create the universe.

I step out beyond the house
And see a blue light
Against my bare arms,
These arms of alabaster.
No arms could be as weak.

I pretend to be a tree
Outstretched above the yard;
Hair spread out after
A fresh rain.

I am told no poem can be created
Outside of Paris.

I burn under this brutal light
As I walk among the trees
In this moon-filled night.

The Soul
and
the Hawk

While driving home from work one afternoon on Interstate 80, I noticed a gray car ahead of me in the middle lane. The car was driving at a much slower speed than the rest of the traffic. I quickly caught up, pulled over into the fast lane, and passed the slow-moving vehicle.

It was driven by a young woman. I looked in my rearview mirror and noticed that she was looking upward. I had to quickly return to my driving, and then I, too, looked up in the sky toward the direction the woman seemed interested in.

There it was, the moon, the full, round moon in the late afternoon, looking gray, flat, and wide.

In the winter, when I drive back and forth to work, I often see a large hawk sitting in a bare tree. It is easy to spot from a distance because its white breast feathers are pronounced against the browns and grays of the dull, empty winter woods. I sometimes pull my car over to the side of the highway, roll down my window, stick my head out, and stare up toward the single hawk. I like to watch as it turns its head back and forth, looking at me, wondering perhaps at my blue car, standing out among all it sees from its perch.

Once I called out to the hawk. "Hello there, in your tree."

In ancient Egypt, the hawk was a symbol for the soul. Where is the soul? They say that our bodies are ninety percent water. What is left? Bone? Hair? Skin cells and a collection of different organs? Perhaps my soul is in the trees with the hawk when I am with the hawk as we call out to each other.

Perhaps my soul was with the young woman as she and I both took quick notice of the gray moon rising in the approaching dusk.

There is an image that haunts me. It is of a small boy running out of church in his blue coat. The coat had a red lining and a hood. Beyond the church, there was a wide path, which led to the cars. I can see this boy running ahead of me. I can see his unbuttoned coat bouncing upon his back. I can see a glimpse of the red lining in his coat. I see his hood popping up and down.

What is strange is that I was the boy, and I knew that I was watching myself, though I cannot explain how this was. A week does not go by in my life when I do not see the image of that running boy.

Every now and then I have this feeling that the physical person that I am is being observed from the outside by someone who is also myself, but from a distance. How is that possible?

We are held together by physical principles: molecules, atoms, DNA, energy. But how can I explain those things that don't seem to follow the regular order of a physical existence?

We all see the moon. We all, at one time or another, recognize in the moon a pull toward a distant space that offers us a moment's grace and a certainty that we are going to be OK.

The
Snow
House

Many years ago, my aunt gave me a glass ball filled with water, and a snowman the size of my thumb. If you turned the sphere upside down, it would begin to "snow" around the little man in the stovepipe hat.

It has been on my desk for over thirty years. When I am stuck on a word, or when I lean back against my chair in exhaustion, I reach over sometimes and shake the glass and watch the snowman disappear in the blizzard.

Am I the lost snowman sometimes being shaken into nothingness?

During one of my winter holidays when I was a college student, I decided to disappear for the week and drive to the cabin in Ontario, Canada, that my father built in 1960.

I had never been to the cabin in winter. I was told it was not suitable for winter habitation, but I wanted to go anyway. My grades in school were poor, I couldn't tell what my future would bring; I was restless.

After a fifteen-hour drive in my 1968 Ford Falcon, which had only one snow tire, I began the final climb up the long dirt road wedged between seven-foot walls of plowed snow.

Some friends in town gave me firewood and a bit of advice.

"Chris, that cabin doesn't have any insulation. You'd be crazy to try and spend the night there."

The car slid back and forth up the dark hill. After my two-mile drive, I pulled over to the side, stepped out, opened the trunk, and lifted out a load of wood.

I could see through the darkness the small cabin's silhouette in the middle of an open field. Each summer, it is great fun to run to the cabin, open it up for the first time since the year before, raise all the windows, make the beds, stack the summer groceries on the shelves.

That dark winter night, I just wanted to step quickly into the house and start a fire in the potbellied stove.

It felt strange to be inside this cabin without my brothers and sisters, without my parents. I closed the door and dropped the wood at the mouth of the stove.

Pulling a flashlight out of my coat pocket, I explored the walls, the closets, the ceiling. As the light passed the dark window, I saw that it was beginning to snow outside.

I opened the stove, stuffed it with small sticks and newspapers and a single log the size of my thigh. I lit the fire and watched the small flame work its way up toward the dried wood.

I pulled open a lawn chair and sat before the fire. No matter how close I sat to the red-hot stove, I could not lose the chill in my body.

Of course I had no business being in a summer cabin in the middle of a Canadian winter, but I wanted to be in that cabin, away from school, my family, the lost memories, the loneliness, and the fear of an uncertain future.

After I discovered that there would be no increase in the house's heat, I stupidly thought that if I curled myself into a ball of blankets, I could sleep comfortably for the night. I pulled out two quilts, dropped the pillows from the couch beside the fire, and placed my body as close to the stove as possible. I was a lonely teenager huddled beside an iron stove, searching for a warmth I could not invoke.

Outside, it snowed and snowed.

By two o'clock in the morning, I still hadn't fallen asleep. I was that cold and that lucky. I could have slept and rolled into the burning stove, or I could have frozen to death.

I crawled out from under the quilts, opened the door, scooped up snow, and threw it into the fire. I listened to the hissing of the wet wood as the flames quickly turned to smoke, and the fire was dead.

I closed the flue, picked up my bag, and stepped out into the darkness. I had to walk past the well, under the crab apple tree, along the path to the car. The snow fell upon my head, against my face, swirling around me as I pressed by boots through the drifts.

Fortunately, the car started, the road was still passable, and I drove twelve miles to the nearest hotel.

I remember that I tried once to break the glass ball my aunt gave me. I wanted to have the snowman, hold it in my hand, keep it on my shelf. I dropped the snow shaker onto the carpet, but the snowman simply hit the inner walls of the globe and disappeared into the swirling "snow." I looked closely and could just see his hat, which was chipped around the top rim.

This year I turn forty-four and see myself disappearing more and more into all that is being stirred up around me: the waning years of this century, my own time spent, a new question of faith. I have repeatedly been asking myself a simple question: "Who is shaking the glass ball?"

I sometimes wish I could penetrate the invisible walls that surround me and drive back to that winter house and drape myself again at the mouth of the hot iron stove.

Hints of

Things to Come

Many years ago, I sat in the front seat of the bookmobile. Mary Anne Gilmore drove the truck. Mary Anne was a staff worker from Madonna House, the rural apostolate in Combermere, Ontario, Canada.

Catherine de Hueck Doherty, founder of Madonna House, believed in the power of the written word. From the very early days of the apostolate, Catherine, known as "B," asked for book donations, established a library for her young staff, and felt a keen responsibility to give local people access to a whole range of books where there was no library.

One summer morning, Mary Anne asked me if I'd like to join her on one of her weekly runs though the backcountry in the bookmobile. I was ten years old and felt very important: An adult wanted *me* as her companion on this important mission.

I remember that the truck was a bit top-heavy, swaying back and forth as we lumbered along the dirt roads, driving from farm to farm with the collection of books to lend. I rested my elbow upon the open windowsill and felt like a prince being escorted through the deep pine barrens of central Canada.

It began to rain. Mary Anne turned the switch for the windshield wipers. I rolled up my window. After a few moments of the heavy downpour, the road started to turn into mud. The truck began a slow ascent, losing power quickly as the gears groaned into place and the wheels spun.

As we reached the summit of the hill, I saw, shooting straight down ahead of us, a narrow dirt driveway that led to a single-story brown house, which sat alone like the dot at the end of an exclamation point.

"Our last stop," Mary Anne said as she placed her foot on the brake pedal and began to ease down the slippery driveway. That is when I noticed two children and a man bending over rows of plants in the distant field to our left.

The windows in the truck were fogged. Mary Anne wiped the inside of her window, giving us a better view. Yes, a boy about my age and a girl about the age of my younger sister.

"What are they doing in the rain?" I asked.

"Tending to the fields, Christopher."

"But it's raining."

Mary Anne gave the truck's horn two quick blasts. The children raised their heads from their labor, looked in our direction, and then began to run toward the house. They wore no shoes. The man, surely their father, also looked our way; then he returned to his labor.

As Mary Anne stopped the truck at the front of the house, a woman stepped out onto the porch, just as the two children leaped over a fence and stood suddenly still behind the truck.

"I got a book to return," the girl called out and ran into the house. She returned with a copy of *The Secret Garden*.

After Mary Anne opened the back door of the truck, the two children stepped up the little ladder that was provided. They disappeared between the two narrow shelves of books. The mother invited Mary Anne and me in for something to drink.

"It's the best water in town. Our well never goes dry."

The interior of the house seemed to be made of loose boards. The chairs didn't match; the sofa looked like a dead elephant. But there was the smell of baked bread; the curtains were blue, and the water was, indeed, delicious.

"I got *The Wizard of Oz* this time," the little girl said as she exploded into the house.

"Wipe your feet. Didn't you already read that?" her mother asked.

"Twice," the girl said as she scraped the mud off her toes against the braided rug.

I looked out the front door and saw that the boy was already halfway across the field, heading out toward his father.

We all seek solace from different sources: perhaps in a novel, perhaps working side by side with a father, perhaps kneading the bread dough.

As Mary Anne and I drove back up the steep driveway, with the books weighing the truck down into the mud and heavy rain, I knew that I wanted to become a teacher.

The Unsubstantial Image

I have seen the image of a beached humpbacked whale slumped on its side, dry, dead, displaced upon the sand, out of the water and in a world it could not possibly understand or endure.

James Joyce is like this whale, or perhaps my students who read his *Portrait of the Artist as a Young Man* are the whales, swimming toward the killing beach, the death air that they must not breathe.

I am a teacher because I wish to help guide my students toward the living sea.

The novel is about a boy who stumbles through his childhood, remembering the sound a cow makes, and the feel of the beating he received in a private school. The child recalls arguments at the Christmas dinner table, the feeling of emptiness in his heart, a longing for an end to loneliness.

Joyce speaks about the need for companionship, writes about a boy who turned sixteen and tried to find solace in the embrace of a woman who wore loose pink robes and a velvet kiss upon her nights for sale.

I remember reading an essay by Martin Buber in which he spoke about the joy reading afforded him, but that joy could be felt only if he knew that after an evening's reading he could step away from his book and find another human being in his home.

How do we become centered? I watched my father spin some clay once on a potter's wheel. His long hands embraced the wet clay. He kicked the footwheel, which began to turn the base where the clay rested. I liked how my father's long fingers pressed into the top of the spinning clay. A simple push with his thumb, and the clay opened a deep, dark place to support the outer walls.

What is the space pressed out of our existence that will support the outer walls of our physical being? We are all placed upon the potter's wheel, prepared to take on a shape that is given to us.

Does gravity and the spin of the earth create the natural forms? I have often wondered what is the true mechanism that forged the shape of the first rose.

Have you seen the photographs of a child still in its mother's womb? The shape of the head, the ear, the entire child floating in distant fluids. Onward to the sea.

We are given shape and form. We are given names. At one point we confront turmoil: To love? To abandon old truths? Question God? Accept loneliness?

The James Joyce boy "wanted to meet in the real world the unsubstantial image which his soul so constantly beheld." That image does not manifest itself in a mirror. What we see is what has been given to us all along. It is the "unsubstantial image" that we desire. I like to think this mystery is what we pray for, select among the best vegetables in the market, glide upon during a cold winter game upon the ice.

My grandfather dared us children each summer to catch barehanded the brown rabbit that appeared each day beyond the raspberry bushes. No one succeeded.

I imagine sometimes that I am among the children again, crawling upon my belly against the grass as we slowly, slowly approach the stone rabbit until, suddenly, it gives a powerful kick with its legs, jumps beyond the distant rock wall, and disappears once more.

When I lose my peace, I begin to consider a return to my writing for the evening. Sometimes I stand before the closed kitchen door and look out into the dark neighborhood and imagine someone will soon visit. I consider another attempt to catch the brown rabbit. Often I simply sleep, and expect the night's fingers to press against me and mold me into a new shape for the next morning, a shape in a new suspense, and then I hear the potter's wheel being kicked, and I spin again.

Perhaps the whale, too, loses its center, endures turmoil, and zooms off in madness toward the beach in hope of salvation. But we cannot seek solace by turning our backs to what we have come to love, to where we have come to know love. We are not mad whales suffering an imbalance in our inner guidance systems. We men and women understand that a center is essential. We understand a longing. We turn and turn under the moon and under the sun and again under the moon and hope, pray, calculate, or guess that what is beyond our understanding is more powerful than the turmoil and safer than a dry beach.

I extend my body upon the warm sand, listen to the distant ice cream bells.

"Can I have a chocolate cone, Daddy?"

"I want an Italian ice, a blue one."

"Will you come with us, Daddy?" I roll up from the beach, brush the sand from my hips, and walk among my sons and my daughter—I, Gulliver, whale, a simple man on vacation within the circle of my children as I continue to live and write for the unsubstantial image.

E P I L O G U E

I cut the hay up to the barn
And trimmed the last measure with a scythe.
There was no harm in my labor,
Which felt like murder
As I swung my blade to advance my place
Before the yard, to claim
A further range as my success.

Innocence is not the place for rest,
But to cut at the base,
To tie in bales and carry to a dry place.

Earth heals itself.
I seek the old wealth of such power
As I close the barn doors
In this late hour.